Napoleon's Kitchen

Napoleon's Kitchen

Recipes from the
French Emperor's Culinary Legacy

Philine G. Lehmann

Published by Harley Obi LLC/History Cafe Press
339 Tarrytown Road #1006
Elmsford, New York 10523 USA
https://bit.ly/m/HistoryCafePress

For my parents, who never discouraged my non-conformist interests, and my husband, who continues their efforts.

"Everything on earth is soon forgotten, except the opinion we leave imprinted on history."

-Napoleon Bonaparte

Table of Contents

**From Then to Table,
Culinary Time Travels**

Discover food through the lens of history!

I n the realm of gastronomic exploration, where flavors become storytellers and recipes unfold like chapters in a historical novel, *From Then to Table, Culinary Time Travels* beckons you to embark on a remarkable journey through the annals of time. This series, a sensory feast, invites you to discover the epicurean heritage that has shaped societies, bringing to life the diverse and delectable dishes that have graced tables throughout the ages.

Food has always been a portal to the soul of a civilization, a tangible expression of its people's joys, struggles, and triumphs. It has been a silent witness to the evolution of time, a consummate storyteller whispering tales of love, war, innovation, and cultural exchange. In this series, you find yourself exploring recipes and unraveling the threads of history woven into the very fabric of our meals. As you leaf through its volumes, you are not just learning to cook; you are partaking in communion with the spirits of those who came before you.

The inspiration for this series arose from my lifelong passion for experiential history. From an early age, my parents planned small summer vacations around historical topics I would learn about during the following school year. Walking the Boston Freedom Trail or in the footsteps of a soldier at Gettysburg added an invaluable dimension to my education. As a high school history teacher for sixteen years, I designed lessons that continued that tradition within the walls of my classroom. My students needed to understand that history is not one-dimensional but a fantastic human narrative that can be learned and lived through sights, sounds, smells, touches, and tastes. *From Then to Table* is a testament to the belief that food is a vessel for cultural exchange, a reflection of societal values, and a bridge that builds a nexus throughout generations.

As you embark on this gastronomical odyssey, prepare to be transported to the lavish banquets of kings, the bustling markets of ancient cities, and the humble hearths of families. *From Then to Table* invites you to embrace the past with an open heart and an empty stomach, ready to savor the timeless flavors that connect us to our shared human heritage. While adapted for the modern kitchen, these recipes maintain their original historic essence.

Whether you are a seasoned cook, historophile, or simply curious about the origins of your favorite dishes, *From Then to Table, Culinary Time Travels* invites you to partake in a feast of the ages. The table is set, the stories are impatiently waiting, and the flavors of bygone days are ready to be devoured. Join us as we embark on these culinary time travels together and enjoy history as tantalizingly intended...one bite at a time.

Philine G. Lehmann, MA
Curator of Flavorful Histories

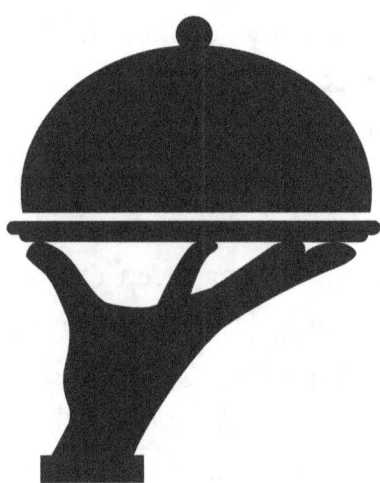

Introduction

"What is a great reputation? A big noise. The more noise you make, the farther it will go. Laws, institutions, monuments, nations, all this passes—but the noise it makes continues to vibrate through other generations."[1]
~ Napoleon Bonaparte ~

N apoleon Bonaparte. Few names in history are illustrious enough to be a sentence in its own right. A formidable French military leader and emperor, he is enshrined in the annals of history for his strategic brilliance, wartime conquests, and enduring impact on European culture. The era of Napoleon stands as a testament to the confluence of power, ambition, and innovation. Yet, amidst the political upheavals and strategic routs, a world of sumptuous indulgence, cultured refinement, and culinary opulence was hidden within the kitchens and banquets of the French Empire. This golden era of unprecedented transformation and enhancement weaved itself intricately into the fabric of social status, power, and cultural identity to the extent that food was no longer mere sustenance but a reflection of one's prestige, an emblem of sophistication, and a tool of diplomacy.

His journey from humble Corsican beginnings to the pinnacle of power in France was accompanied by a discerning yet unassuming palate and an unwavering appreciation for the finer things in life, especially food. Napoleon's tastes blended sophistication and simplicity, reflecting his character and the diverse influences of the regions under his rule. The dishes that graced his table ran the gamut from sumptuous roasts, rich sauces, and decadent desserts to rustic fares like hearty soups or simple omelettes, each meticulously curated to suit his tastes. He surrounded himself with renowned chefs tasked with concocting dishes that would satisfy him and reflect his reign's grandeur. Indeed, behind every military campaign lay a table set with exquisite dishes and fine wines, as Napoleon understood the importance of winning and dining in diplomacy and alliance-building.

To understand the culinary essence of the French Empire, one must appreciate the historical context in which it flourished. The amalgamation of regional flavors, brought together by Napoleon's policies that encouraged the exchange of cultural traditions across the empire, led to the creation of iconic dishes still enjoyed today. The imperial pantry was a treasure trove of luxury ingredients adored by the aristocracy, such as truffles and foie gras, alongside staples such as bread, cheese, and wine consumed by the masses. Likewise, the cooking techniques utilized during this period were equally refined and fundamental. The art of sautéing, braising, and roasting reached new heights, and sauces became a hallmark of French cuisine. Techniques such as roux-based sauces and careful reductions were perfected during this period, laying the foundation for French haute cuisine.

Beyond the battles and treaties, Napoleon's era was a time of remarkable gastronomic innovation, fusion of flavors, and the refinement of French culinary traditions. It offers a glimpse into the gastronomic heritage of Napoleonic France, presenting a curated selection of recipes that reflect the diversity of the era. From Napoleon's favorites to dishes served at grand celebrations in his court, each recipe encapsulates a piece of history waiting to be rediscovered and savored. *Napoleon's Kitchen*—where every dish tells a story, every flavor echoes an emperor's legacy, and every meal is a tribute to an era of unparalleled elegance and refinement.

Bon Appétit!

Chapter Two

The Imperial Pantry
Ingredients that Shaped an Empire

The era of Napoleon Bonaparte was a time of profound transformation in French cuisine. Diverse influences and societal changes that Napoleon ushered in directly impacted his culinary world. The pantry of a French kitchen during Napoleon's time was a treasure trove of luxurious and humble ingredients. This reflected the abundance of riches in France and echoed the empire's global influence and affluence.

The pantry staples permeated with a richness that mirrored the grandeur of the era. Abundant and indulgent butter formed the base of many dishes, elevating flavors and adding a velvety texture to sauces and pastries. Decadent and luxurious creams, applied liberally, transformed simple ingredients into culinary masterpieces fit for royalty. Fine meats held a place of honor on the tables of the empire. From succulent roasts to intricate game dishes, the variety and quality of meats showcased the prowess of French culinary expertise, served with lavish dressings to create unforgettable dining experiences.

During Napoleon's rule, France was a mosaic of culinary traditions, each region contributing unique flavors and techniques to the national cuisine, creating a culinary map that was a tapestry woven with diversity. The sun-kissed landscapes of Provence gifted French cuisine with vibrant herbs, olive oil, and an abundance of seafood. Recipes from this region emphasized freshness and simplicity, celebrating the bounty of the Mediterranean. Normandy's verdant pastures and coastal richness introduced creamy dairy products, succulent apples, and an array of shellfish. Last but certainly not least, Lyon, renowned as the gastronomic capital of France, offered robust and hearty fare, most notably its intricate sauces and charcuterie.

Sauces played a crucial role in French cuisine, reflecting the refinement and artistry of the culinary world. Rich sauces, often prepared with butter, cream, and a myriad of herbs and spices adorned the tables of the elite. Béchamel, *espagnole*, velouté, and hollandaise required meticulous preparation and skilled craftsmanship that not only added flavor but also showcased the prowess of French chefs. The intricate and time-consuming sauce-making process mirrored the sophistication and attention to detail during Napoleon's reign.

Napoleon's conquests and trade expansions introduced exotic spices and ingredients to French kitchens. The interactions between diverse cultures facilitated a melting pot of gastronomic traditions. Fusing flavors and techniques resulted in unique dishes marrying French sophistication and international influences. Trade routes expanded during Napoleon's reign, bringing back spices, herbs, and other Asian ingredients. Widely unfamiliar flavors like saffron, cardamom, cumin, cinnamon, cloves, and nutmeg began to find their place in French kitchens, adding depth and complexity to traditional recipes. These spices, coveted not just for their flavors but for the status they conferred upon those who owned them, became prized culinary possessions.

The Napoleonic campaigns also resulted in integrating new techniques into the culinary repertoire. Italy's deep-rooted traditions, especially pasta and sauces, seamlessly integrated into French cooking, transforming dishes like coq au vin and beef bourguignon. Eastern European influences introduced hearty stews and root vegetables, adding depth and earthiness. Spain's introduction of tomatoes, peppers, and saffron sparked a revolution in flavors, evident in bouillabaisse and ratatouille. The Low Countries contributed techniques in pastry-making, elevating desserts. Scandinavian influences emphasized seafood and pickling methods, enriching dishes like gravlax and enhancing the use of fish. Napoleon's era thus became a melting pot, enriching and diversifying the already esteemed French culinary landscape.

No discussion of the Napoleonic pantry would be complete without mention of the wines and spirits that flowed freely in his court. France's vineyards produced some of the world's finest wines coveted across continents, adorning tables with Bordeaux, Burgundy, and Champagne. These libations were not mere beverages but symbols of refinement, adding elegance to every gathering. Additionally, artistic cocktail-making thrived during the French Empire, with mixologists crafting libations that combined spirits, flavors, and theatrical flair.

The ingredients gracing the imperial pantry were cultural artifacts that defined an era. Even today, their legacy lives on, reminding us of a time when food was more than sustenance, but also a symbol of power, refinement, and the essence of an empire. The conquests of Napoleon introduced Gallic gastronomy to previously untouched regions and simultaneously brought back diverse flavors and cooking techniques that enriched French kitchens. To understand the imperial cuisine, one must appreciate the historical context in which it flourished. The elevation of regional flavors, brought together by Napoleon's policies that encouraged the exchange of traditions, led to the creation of iconic dishes that endure today.

Marie-Antonin Carême (1784-1833) began his culinary career as an apprentice in Paris. His talent quickly gained recognition, and he became the chef to numerous notable figures, such as King George IV of England, Tsar Alexander I of Russia, and Emperor Napoleon Bonaparte. As the emperor's personal chef, Carême used an elaborate pantry to conjure up gastronomic wonders that delighted Napoleon and captivated the most distinguished guests of the time.

Carême transformed and formalized French cooking methods and pioneered haute cuisine. His contributions and elaborate presentations earned him the title "King of Chefs and Chef of Kings." Carême also created classical culinary categories, such as the *Grandes et Petites sauces* (grand and small sauces): velouté, béchamel, allemande, and *espagnole*.

In addition to his accomplishments in the kitchen, Carême wrote several landmark cookbooks, such as *Le Patissier Royal Parisien* and *L'Art de la Cuisine Française au Dix-Neuvième Siècle*. His influence continues today, inspiring chefs who came after him and laying the groundwork for contemporary French cuisine.

Further Reading:
Kelly, Ian. *Cooking for Kings: The Life of Antonin Carême: The First Celebrity Chef.* New York: Walker & Co, 2005.

Chapter Three

Palate of Power
The Culinary Choices of an Emperor

Born in the Mediterranean haven of Corsica, amidst the rugged terrain and aromatic landscapes, Napoleon Bonaparte's gastronomic journey began. His homeland's earthy, robust flavors significantly influenced his palate. The aroma of wild herbs lingered in the air as the young Napoleon roamed the countryside. Here, the essence of Corsican cuisine enveloped his senses. The recipes passed down through generations, steeped in tradition and honoring the bounty of the land and sea, became the cornerstone of his culinary preferences.

The story of Corsican cuisine is a narrative spun over centuries, blending the threads of various civilizations that left their indelible mark on the island's culinary identity. From the ancient Greeks who first cultivated the olive trees to the Romans who introduced vineyards and the subsequent waves of Italian and French influences, each new conquerer added layers to Corsica's gastronomic heritage. Corsican recipes, grounded in simplicity and resourcefulness, drew heavily from the island's natural bounty. The land itself, with its fertile valleys and rocky terrain, provided a diverse array of ingredients—wild herbs (myrtle, juniper, and maquis), chestnuts that found their way into bread and pastries, and the renowned Corsican honey that lent its sweetness to dishes both savory and sweet.

The island's unique blend of flavors found expression in iconic dishes like the hearty and flavorful wild boar stew, *civet de sanglier,* or the delicate *fiadone,* a cheesecake redolent with the aroma of *brocciu,* the Corsican fresh cheese. Seafood was an abundant resource along the coastline and highly cherished. Fishermen brought treasures from the Mediterranean, inspiring dishes like *calamars farcis* (stuffed squid) and *baccalà* (salt cod). The Corsicans' mastery of preserving meats through air-drying and curing birthed delicacies like *lonzu* (cured pork loin) and *prisuttu* (air-dried ham). Culinary techniques passed down through generations involved a profound understanding of the terrain and its offerings. From foraging for aromatic herbs in the maquis to the art of making chestnut flour, Corsican cooking embraced a rustic elegance that celebrated the essence of each ingredient.

As Napoleon ascended to power, his palate reflected the essence of his homeland's simplicity intertwined with a burgeoning sophistication. He retained an affinity for the hearty and robust flavors that characterized his birthplace—a fondness for game meats, wild herbs, and the earthy richness of Corsican cheeses. However, as the corridors of power widened, so did Napoleon's culinary horizons. He embraced the refinement of French cuisine, welcoming the elegance of sauces and delicate pastries while maintaining a penchant for the unpretentious dishes reminiscent of his heritage. Napoleon's dining habits were a testament to his multi-faceted tastes. Lavish banquets showcased the grandeur of French culinary artistry, while intimate meals often featured dishes that harkened back to the rustic flavors of Corsica, creating a nuanced tableau of tastes.

Amidst the magnificence of imperial feasts, the flavors of Corsica found their way onto Napoleon's table, courtesy of chefs who understood his appreciation for the tastes of his youth. Corsican ingredients—chestnuts, maquis herbs, *brocciu*, and wild game—cleverly integrated into courtly dishes, a subtle homage to Napoleon's roots. *Civet de sanglier* made occasional appearances, the aroma of juniper and myrtle infusing the air, while brocciu found its way into delicate pastries, adding a touch of familiarity to the refined desserts served in the imperial court.

Accounts from witnesses and historical records offer a glimpse into the emperor's distinctive eating rituals. Anecdotes abound about Napoleon's preference for small, swift meals, often consumed hastily amid his packed schedule—a stark contrast to the lavish banquets he hosted out of necessity. Due to the speed at which he swallowed his food, attendants wondered if he even chewed. He often ate with his fingers. Despite his choice of utensils, or seeming lack thereof, and his unconventional table manners, Napoleon reportedly demanded fastidiousness in etiquette, at least for everyone else. He preferred a quiet and orderly meal, disliking chaos or commotion during dining. Stories also circulated about the emperor's tendency to avoid eating in the presence of others, favoring solitary meals to maintain focus or to avoid discomfort in social settings. There were a few occasions during his reign when he ate *dîner en grand couvert* (a custom where royal dinners were open to the public). Those were only for events of significant import, and he quickly abandoned the weekly Sunday tradition.

His mornings commenced with a strong cup of coffee. Occasionally, he would partake in an item from the *petit-déjeuner* (breakfast) spread, but his first proper meal arrived during *déjeuner* (lunch), served on his schedule and usually for him alone. They were simple affairs, as opposed to those more traditionally enjoyed by the citizenry of his class during the time. During *déjeuner*, Napoleon often entertained his children and his nieces and nephews. He also engaged intellectuals, artists of varying fields, and officers. Various accounts profess the sentiment that *déjeuner* was a rare experience, as this was when Napoleon allowed his true self to manifest unadulterated. According to Napoleon's valet, Constant:

> "However near you saw him, the Emperor was always a *hero*, but you also gained much from seeing the *man* close up and in detail. From afar, you felt only the prestige of his power and glory, but as you approached you were surprised to find yourself enjoying, too, all the charm of his conversation, all of the simplicity of his family life, and —I do not hesitate to say it—the ingrained benevolence of his character."[2]

It was amidst the splendor of *dîner* (dinner) feasts that his culinary preferences exhibited themselves. Surrounded by close confidants and esteemed guests, Napoleon's table became a stage for gastronomic delights, with often upwards of twenty different dishes presented at a time to afford variety and choice. Despite the copious amount of food available, Napoleon continued his tradition of eating quickly and often abruptly left the table before his guests finished. A workaholic, Napoleon frequently arrived late to *dîner*, and his family typically ate without him.

Despite the extravagance that surrounded him, he found solace in the humble flavors of Corsican cuisine reminiscent of his roots. He cherished dishes like *aziminu*, a hearty vegetable soup, and *fiadone*, a traditional cheesecake, as a reminder of his humble beginnings. Records suggest that Napoleon was fond of poultry, particularly chicken and turkey dishes. Additionally, historical references hint at Napoleon's enjoyment of various sweets and pastries, showcasing a penchant for indulgent desserts. Accounts attest to his fondness for éclairs, and he enjoyed their delicate sweetness as a rare treat amidst the rigors of his campaigns. While the emperor's culinary indulgences varied, they offered a glimpse into the human side of Napoleon—a man with tastes and cravings that transcended the demands of his leadership.

Further Reading:

Constant, Louis. *Memoirs of Constant, First Valet de Chambre of the Emperor, on the Private Life of Napoleon, His Family and His Court; 2 Volumes.* Legare Street Press, 2023.

Emmanuel-Auguste-Dieudonné Las Cases. *Memorial de Sainte Helene: Journal of the Private Life and Conversations of the Emperor Napoleon at Saint Helena.* Legare Street Press, 2022.

Gregorovius, Ferdinand. *Corsica: Picturesque, Historical, and Social: With a Sketch of the Early Life of Napoleon, and an Account of the Bonaparte, Paoli, Pozzo Di Borgo, and Other Principal Families.* Translated by E.J. Morris. London: British Library Historical Prints, 2011.

Louis-Etienne Saint-Denis. *Napoleon from the Tuileries to St. Helena.* Legare Street Press, 2022.

Marchand, Louis-Joseph. *In Napoleon's Shadow.* Barnsley, England: Casemate Publishers, 2018.

Civet de Sanglier

This distinctive Wild Boar Stew captures the essence of Corsican cuisine, blending the bold flavors of Corsican wine, aromatic maquis herbs, and tender wild boar chunks. Slow-cooked to perfection, this hearty dish pays homage to the island's rich culinary traditions, delivering a savory symphony that promises to transport your taste buds to the sun-soaked hills of Corsica.

Ingredients

- 2 pounds (about 1 kg) wild boar meat, cut into chunks
- 1 bottle red wine (preferably Corsican wine or a robust red wine)
- 2 onions, finely chopped
- 2 carrots, peeled and diced
- 4 cloves garlic, minced
- 2 tablespoons olive oil
- 2 tablespoons all-purpose flour
- 2 bay leaves
- 4 sprigs thyme
- 2 cups game stock (or beef stock)
- Salt and black pepper to taste
- 1 tablespoon tomato paste
- 1 tablespoon red wine vinegar
- 1 tablespoon Corsican maquis herbs (a mixture of aromatic herbs like rosemary, thyme, oregano)
- Butter or lard for cooking

Instructions

1. Place the wild boar meat in a large bowl and pour the Corsican or robust red wine over it. Let it marinate for at least 12 hours or overnight in the refrigerator.

2. After marinating, drain the meat and reserve the wine.

3. In a large, heavy-bottomed pot, heat the olive oil over medium-high heat. Add the wild boar chunks and brown them on all sides. Remove the meat and set it aside.

4. In the same pot, add a bit more oil if needed, then sauté the onions, carrots, and garlic until softened.

5. Sprinkle the flour over the vegetables and stir to coat them. This will help thicken the stew.

6. Return the browned wild boar to the pot. Pour in the reserved Corsican or red wine, game stock (or beef stock), and add the bay leaves, thyme, and Corsican maquis herbs. Season with salt and black pepper.

7. Add the tomato paste and red wine vinegar. Stir well to combine.

8. Bring the stew to a boil, then reduce the heat to low, cover, and let it simmer for at least 2-3 hours or until the wild boar is tender. You can also transfer the pot to a preheated oven at 325°F (163°C) and cook it there.

9. Check the seasoning and adjust if necessary before serving.

10. Serve the Civet de Sanglier hot with crusty bread, polenta, or over a bed of cooked rice.

Fiadone

This classic Corsican cheesecake is a symphony of creamy ricotta, citrusy zest, and a buttery crust that encapsulates the essence of the Mediterranean. A simple yet elegant dessert, Fiadone invites you to experience the sweet flavors of Corsica, beautifully wrapped in a golden pastry shell. With each velvety bite, savor the harmonious balance of textures and the distinctive notes of lemon and orange that make this treat a cherished delight.

Ingredients

For the Pastry

- 2 cups all-purpose flour
- 1/2 cup unsalted butter, cold and diced
- 1/2 cup granulated sugar
- 1 large egg
- A pinch of salt

For the Filling

- 2 cups ricotta cheese
- 1 cup sugar
- 4 large eggs
- Zest of 1 lemon
- Zest of 1 orange
- 1 teaspoon vanilla extract

Optional Toppings

- Confectioners' sugar for dusting
- Sliced almonds for garnish

Instructions

Pastry

1. In a large mixing bowl, combine the flour, cold diced butter, sugar, egg, and a pinch of salt.

2. Use your fingertips to rub the ingredients together until the mixture resembles breadcrumbs.

3. Form the dough into a ball, wrap it in plastic wrap, and refrigerate for at least 30 minutes.

4. Preheat your oven to 350°F (175°C).

5. Roll out the pastry on a floured surface to fit a greased tart pan. Press the pastry into the pan, ensuring an even layer on the bottom and up the sides. Trim any excess dough.

Filling

1. In a separate bowl, mix the ricotta cheese, sugar, eggs, lemon zest, orange zest, and vanilla extract until smooth.

2. Pour the ricotta mixture into the prepared pastry shell.

3. Optional: Sprinkle sliced almonds on top for a crunchy texture.

4. Bake in the preheated oven for about 40-45 minutes or until the filling is set and the top is golden brown.

5. Allow the Fiadone to cool completely before refrigerating for at least 2 hours.

6. Once chilled, dust the top with confectioners' sugar for a finishing touch. Slice and serve.

Aziminu

Prepare to transport your taste buds to the shores of Corsica as you enjoy the warmth and richness of this traditional fish soup. This savory delight features a medley of fresh seafood, including fish fillets, mussels, clams, and shrimp, simmered in a flavorful broth infused with aromatic vegetables and a touch of white wine. Served hot and garnished with fresh parsley, Aziminu invites you to savor the essence of the Mediterranean, delivering a comforting and satisfying experience with every spoonful.

Ingredients

- 1 lb (about 450g) mixed fish fillets (such as red snapper, sea bass, or monkfish), cut into chunks
- 1/2 lb (about 225g) mussels, cleaned and debearded
- 1/2 lb (about 225g) clams, scrubbed
- 1/2 lb (about 225g) shrimp, peeled and deveined
- 1/4 cup olive oil
- 1 large onion, finely chopped
- 2 leeks, white and light green parts only, sliced
- 2 carrots, peeled and diced
- 2 tomatoes, chopped
- 4 garlic cloves, minced
- 1 fennel bulb, sliced
- 1 cup dry white wine
- 6 cups fish or seafood stock
- 1 bay leaf
- 1 teaspoon dried thyme
- Salt and black pepper to taste
- Fresh parsley, chopped, for garnish
- Crusty bread for serving

Instructions

1. In a large pot, heat the olive oil over medium heat. Add the chopped onion, leeks, and carrots. Sauté until the vegetables are softened.

2. Add the minced garlic and sliced fennel to the pot. Continue cooking for a few more minutes until fragrant.

3. Pour in the white wine and allow it to simmer for a couple of minutes, letting the alcohol evaporate.

4. Add the chopped tomatoes, bay leaf, and dried thyme to the pot. Stir well.

5. Pour in the fish or seafood stock, bring the mixture to a boil, then reduce the heat to simmer. Let it simmer for about 15-20 minutes, allowing the flavors to meld.

6. Season the broth with salt and black pepper to taste.

7. Add the fish fillets, mussels, clams, and shrimp to the pot. Simmer until the seafood is cooked through and the mussel and clam shells have opened. Discard any unopened shells.

8. Remove the bay leaf from the soup.

9. Serve the Aziminu hot, garnished with fresh parsley. Accompany it with crusty bread for a complete and satisfying meal.

Caldarroste

Caldarroste, or roasted chestnuts, is a delightful Italian treat often enjoyed during the fall and winter. As the air turns crisp, the simple pleasure of warm, oven-roasted chestnuts offers a delightful and aromatic treat. With a touch of rustic elegance, this recipe captures the essence of autumn and winter gatherings.

Ingredients

- Fresh chestnuts (as many as desired)
- Water for soaking

Instructions

1. Preheat your oven to 425°F (220°C). Using a sharp knife, make a small incision or an "X" on the flat side of each chestnut. This helps prevent them from exploding during roasting.

2. Place the chestnuts in a bowl and cover them with water. Let them soak for about 15-20 minutes. While the chestnuts are soaking, prepare a baking sheet by lining it with parchment paper.

3. After soaking, drain the chestnuts and pat them dry with a towel. Arrange the chestnuts on the prepared baking sheet, ensuring they are in a single layer.

4. Roast the chestnuts in the preheated oven for about 20-25 minutes, or until the outer shells have split and the inner flesh is tender.

5. Remove the chestnuts from the oven and let them cool slightly before handling. Once the chestnuts are cool enough to touch, peel away the outer shell and the thin inner skin, revealing the creamy, roasted chestnut inside.

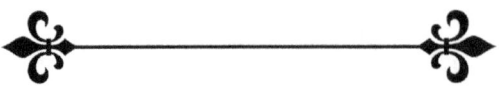

Panzarotti

These fried calzones, filled with a savory blend of ricotta, mozzarella, and Parmesan, offer a taste of authentic Italian street food right from your kitchen. Perfectly golden and irresistibly delicious, Panzarotti are a joy to make and savor. Whether enjoyed as a snack or a crowd-pleasing appetizer, this recipe promises a burst of flavor and a satisfying crunch with each bite.

Ingredients

Dough

- 3 cups all-purpose flour
- 1 teaspoon sugar
- 1 teaspoon salt
- 1 tablespoon active dry yeast
- 1 cup warm water (110°F/43°C)
- 2 tablespoons olive oil

Filling

- 1 cup ricotta cheese
- 1 cup shredded mozzarella cheese
- 1/2 cup grated Parmesan cheese
- 1 egg
- 1 tablespoon fresh parsley, chopped
- Salt and black pepper to taste
- Optional: Cooked and crumbled Italian sausage, sautéed mushrooms, or other desired fillings

Other

- Vegetable oil for frying
- Marinara sauce for dipping

Instructions

Dough

1. In a bowl, combine warm water and sugar. Stir until the sugar dissolves, then sprinkle the yeast over the water. Let it sit for about 5 minutes until the yeast becomes foamy.

2. In a large mixing bowl, combine the flour and salt. Make a well in the center and pour in the yeast mixture and olive oil.

3. Mix the ingredients until a dough forms. Knead the dough on a floured surface for about 5-7 minutes until it becomes smooth and elastic. Place the dough in a lightly oiled bowl, cover it with a damp cloth, and let it rise in a warm place for 1-2 hours or until it doubles in size.

Filling

In a bowl, combine ricotta, mozzarella, Parmesan, egg, chopped parsley, salt, and black pepper. Mix until well combined. Optionally, add desired fillings such as cooked Italian sausage or sautéed mushrooms.

Assembly

1. Preheat vegetable oil in a deep fryer or a heavy pot to 375°F (190°C).

2. Punch down the risen dough and divide it into golf ball-sized portions. Roll out each portion into a small round disc (about 4-5 inches in diameter).

3. Place a spoonful of the cheese filling in the center of each disc. Fold the dough over the filling, sealing the edges by pressing with a fork.

Frying

1. Carefully place the sealed Panzarotti into the hot oil, a few at a time, and fry until golden brown on both sides (about 3-4 minutes).

2. Remove the Panzarotti with a slotted spoon and drain on paper towels.

3. Serve the Panzarotti hot with marinara sauce for dipping.

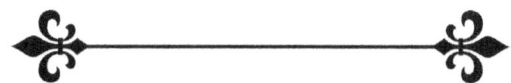

Pasta alla Bastiaccia

This delightful Corsican pasta dish combines the essence of the island's flavors, marrying ground meat with a robust tomato and red wine sauce infused with aromatic Corsican herbs. As the savory aroma fills your kitchen, you will be anticipating the moment you savor each forkful of pasta coated in this rich and hearty sauce. Topped with grated Pecorino or Parmesan cheese and optional fresh herbs, Pasta alla Bastiaccia is a celebration of Corsican culinary traditions that invites you to experience the warmth and authenticity of Mediterranean cuisine in every delicious bite.

Ingredients

- 1 pound (about 450g) pasta (penne, fusilli, or your choice)
- 1/4 cup olive oil
- 1 onion, finely chopped
- 2 cloves garlic, minced
- 1 pound (about 450g) ground meat (beef or a mixture of beef and pork)
- 1 can (14 oz) crushed tomatoes
- 1/2 cup red wine
- 1 teaspoon dried Corsican herbs (a mix of rosemary, thyme, oregano)
- Salt and black pepper to taste
- Grated Pecorino or Parmesan cheese for serving
- Fresh basil or parsley for garnish (optional)

Instructions

1. Cook the pasta according to the package instructions until al dente. Drain and set aside.

2. In a large skillet, heat olive oil over medium heat. Add the chopped onion and cook until softened.

3. Add minced garlic to the skillet and sauté for another minute until fragrant.

4. Add the ground meat to the skillet, breaking it up with a spoon. Cook until browned.

5. Pour in the red wine and allow it to simmer for a few minutes, letting the alcohol evaporate.

6. Stir in the crushed tomatoes and dried Corsican herbs. Season with salt and black pepper to taste.

7. Simmer the sauce over low heat for about 15-20 minutes, allowing the flavors to meld.

8. Toss the cooked pasta into the skillet, coating it evenly with the sauce.

9. Serve Pasta alla Bastiaccia hot, garnished with grated Pecorino or Parmesan cheese.

10. Optionally, add fresh basil or parsley for a burst of freshness.

Stufatu

This traditional Corsican dish invites you to savor tender beef cubes, slow-cooked to perfection, in a rich combination of red wine, crushed tomatoes, and aromatic herbs. The result is a robust and comforting stew, where each bite reflects the island's culinary heritage. Garnished with fresh parsley, this Stufatu promises a symphony of flavors that will transport you to the sun-kissed shores of Corsica with every spoonful. Immerse yourself in the warmth and depth of this authentic Mediterranean delight.

Ingredients

- 2 pounds (about 1 kg) beef stew meat, cut into cubes
- 4 tablespoons olive oil
- 2 onions, finely chopped
- 4 cloves garlic, minced
- 2 carrots, peeled and sliced
- 2 celery stalks, sliced
- 1 cup red wine (Corsican wine or a robust red wine)
- 1 can (14 oz) crushed tomatoes
- 1 cup beef or vegetable broth
- 2 bay leaves
- 2 sprigs rosemary
- 2 sprigs thyme
- Salt and black pepper to taste
- 1 tablespoon tomato paste
- 1 tablespoon flour (optional, for thickening)
- Chopped fresh parsley for garnish

Instructions

1. In a large pot or Dutch oven, heat 2 tablespoons of olive oil over medium-high heat. Brown the beef cubes in batches until they are well-seared on all sides. Set aside.

2. In the same pot, add the remaining 2 tablespoons of olive oil. Sauté the chopped onions, minced garlic, carrots, and celery until softened.

3. Sprinkle the flour over the vegetables and stir to coat, providing a thickening agent for the stew (optional).

4. Return the browned beef to the pot. Pour in the red wine, scraping the bottom to release any flavorful bits.

5. Add the crushed tomatoes, beef or vegetable broth, bay leaves, rosemary, thyme, salt, and black pepper. Stir in the tomato paste.

6. Bring the stew to a gentle boil, then reduce the heat to low, cover, and simmer for about 2-3 hours or until the beef is tender. Stir occasionally.

7. Check the seasoning and adjust as needed. If the stew needs thickening, you can mix a bit more flour with water and stir it into the pot.

8. Discard the bay leaves, rosemary, and thyme sprigs.

9. Serve the Stufatu hot, garnished with chopped fresh parsley. It pairs well with crusty bread, rice, or potatoes.

Salad with Maquis Herbs

Elevate your salad experience with this Salad with Maquis Herbs recipe, a vibrant homage to the aromatic and flavorful essence of Corsica. This refreshing dish combines a medley of mixed greens, cherry tomatoes, crisp cucumber, red onion, black olives, and crumbled feta cheese, adorned with the distinctive charm of Corsican herbs. The Maquis Herb Vinaigrette, with its blend of rosemary, thyme, and oregano, adds a fragrant and savory touch, creating a salad that transports your palate to the sun-kissed landscapes of the Mediterranean. Whether enjoyed as a light meal or a delightful side, this salad promises freshness and the unmistakable allure of Corsican culinary traditions.

Ingredients

For the Salad

- Mixed salad greens (arugula, watercress, baby spinach)
- Cherry tomatoes, halved
- Cucumbers, sliced
- Red onion, thinly sliced
- Feta cheese, crumbled
- Kalamata olives

For the Maquis Herb Dressing

- 1/4 cup extra virgin olive oil
- 2 tablespoons red wine vinegar
- 1 teaspoon Dijon mustard
- 1 clove garlic, minced
- 1 tablespoon Corsican herb blend (rosemary, thyme, oregano)
- Salt and black pepper to taste

Optional Additions

- Grilled chicken or shrimp for protein
- Toasted pine nuts for extra crunch

Instructions

Maquis Herb Dressing

1. In a small bowl, whisk together extra virgin olive oil, red wine vinegar, Dijon mustard, minced garlic, and Corsican herb blend.

2. Season the dressing with salt and black pepper to taste. Set aside to let the flavors meld.

Salad Assembly

1. In a large salad bowl, combine the mixed salad greens, cherry tomatoes, sliced cucumbers, red onion, crumbled feta cheese, and Kalamata olives.

2. If desired, add grilled chicken or shrimp for a protein boost.

3. Drizzle the Maquis Herb Dressing over the salad and toss gently to coat the ingredients evenly.

4. Sprinkle toasted pine nuts on top for an extra crunch.

5. Serve the Maquis Herb Salad immediately, enjoying the vibrant flavors of the Corsican herbs and fresh ingredients.

Chapter Four

Sunrise in the Empire
Breakfasts

In the quiet hours of dawn, amidst the opulent courts of France and the bustling streets of its cities, a ritual unfolded that would shape not only the day but also the very fabric of society. Breakfast was a meal that varied significantly between the classes. For the privileged few, it was an opportunity to indulge in luxurious flavors and elaborate presentations. At the same time, for the common folk, it often consisted of simple yet hearty fare to kickstart the day's labor. During the era of Napoleon, a period marked by grandeur, revolution, and transformation, breakfast held a profound significance far beyond its sustenance value.

Breakfast was a telling marker of social status. In the opulent salons of the aristocracy, mornings commenced with elaborate spreads—decadent pastries, exotic fruits, and delicacies procured from distant lands. The nobility's breakfast was a spectacle where abundance and refinement intermingled, showcasing wealth and power. For the masses, in contrast, it was comprised of a more straightforward fare. Bread, butter, and perhaps a humble bowl of porridge were staples, representing sustenance rather than extravagance. The divide between classes was palpable, even in how they broke their fast.

As the sun rose over the empire, breakfast table settings precisely reflected the nuances of class, tradition, and innovation that defined this momentous era. It was not merely a meal but a mirror that reflected the multifaceted layers of the time—its ingredients, rituals, and the cultural landscape that shaped its essence. From the lavish feasts of nobility to the modest gatherings of commoners, breakfast was a prism through which societal structures, political intrigues, and personal preferences converged.

The foundation of breakfast lay in the staples cultivated across the French countryside. Wheat and rye flourished in the fields, forming the backbone of bread—the cornerstone of the meal for the aristocracy and commoners alike. The art of breadmaking ascended to an artisanal craft, yielding a wide array, from crusty baguettes to delicate brioche. Beyond grains, dairy played a pivotal role. Butter, milk, and cheeses, sourced from the pastoral landscapes dotting the country, also graced the morning table.

France's diverse regions contributed distinct flavors and culinary traditions to the morning table. The coastal areas offered seafood delights, such as oysters and smoked fish, that adorned maritime community breakfast feasts. Inland regions brought forth hearty fare—sausages, potatoes, and eggs cooked in various styles—reflecting the bounty of the countryside. From the lavish spreads of Parisian salons to the rustic simplicity of rural kitchens, regional variations painted a vibrant mosaic of flavors and ingredients that graced tables nationwide.

The breakfast landscape in Napoleonic France was not static, and the passage of time brought subtle yet discernible shifts in habits. The aftermath of the French Revolution saw a departure from opulence, favoring simplicity and practicality. As the 19th century unfolded, industrialization and urbanization altered lifestyles, impacting choices. Convenience became paramount, leading to the rise of quicker options for the burgeoning urban populace. Moreover, the middle class began to assert its influence, shaping preferences that balanced practicality with aspirations for refinement. Breakfast, once a marker of social hierarchy, became a more democratized meal, reflecting changing societal norms.

Colonial expeditions and trade routes brought exotic ingredients and culinary practices from distant lands, enriching the breakfast table with newfound flavors. Coffee, introduced through this avenue, became a ubiquitous morning beverage, rivaling traditional tea and hot chocolate. Furthermore, interactions with neighboring countries and regions led to exchanges, resulting in the assimilation of foreign breakfast elements into French cuisine. This fusion contributed to the diversity of offerings and expanded the palates of the populace.

From the opulent tables of the elite to the humble kitchens of commoners, each morning repast reflected the societal tapestry and culinary craftsmanship of a remarkable time. This collection of recipes invites you to savor the essence of Napoleonic breakfasts, offering a tantalizing glimpse into the ingredients, techniques, and flavors that graced tables during a period marked by grandeur, revolution, and the artistry of French cuisine.

Classic French Croissants

The allure of a perfect croissant—crisp, golden, and delicately layered—has transcended time and borders, becoming a symbol of French pastry craftsmanship. The history of the croissant intertwines with tales of Viennese bakers and Turkish crescents, but it found its place of honor in French patisseries during Napoleon's era. Legend has it that the emperor, enamored by its flaky layers and buttery richness, made croissants a morning ritual, indulging in their exquisite taste as he strategized his conquests.

Ingredients

- 4 cups all-purpose flour, plus extra for dusting
- ¼ cup granulated sugar
- 2 teaspoons salt
- 1 ¼ cups cold water
- 1 tablespoon active dry yeast
- 1 cup unsalted butter, chilled and cut into thin slices

Instructions

1. Prepare the Dough

- In a mixing bowl, combine the flour, sugar, and salt. Dissolve the yeast in the cold water and add it to the dry ingredients. Mix until a dough forms.
- Knead the dough on a lightly floured surface for about 10 minutes until smooth. Shape it into a ball, cover with plastic wrap, and refrigerate for 1 hour.

2. Incorporate the Butter

- On a floured surface, roll out the chilled dough into a rectangle. Place the slices of chilled butter evenly over two-thirds of the dough. Fold the unbuttered third over the buttered middle third, then fold the opposite end over the top, creating three layers.
- Rotate the dough 90 degrees, roll it out into a rectangle again, and repeat the folding process. Wrap the dough in plastic wrap and refrigerate for 30 minutes.

3. Shape and Bake

- Preheat the oven to 400°F (200°C). Roll out the dough into a large rectangle, about ¼ inch thick. Cut triangles of dough and roll them up from the base to the tip to create crescent shapes.
- Place the croissants on a baking sheet lined with parchment paper. Let them rise in a warm place for 1-2 hours until doubled in size.
- Bake for 15-18 minutes or until the croissants are golden brown and puffed up. Serve warm.

Serving Suggestions and Variations

- Enjoy freshly baked croissants with a spread of homemade preserves or high-quality French butter.

Variations:
- *Pain au Chocolat: Encase a piece of dark chocolate in the dough before rolling to create a chocolate-filled variation.
- *Almond Croissants: Brush baked croissants with simple syrup and sprinkle sliced almonds for a crunchy twist.

Further Reading:
Chevallier, Jim. *August Zang and the French Croissant*. Amazon Publishing, 2009.

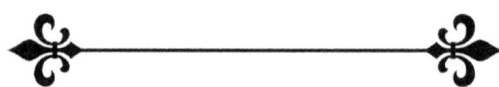

Omelette à la Provençale

This classic French omelette captures the essence of the region's vibrant flavors, combining farm-fresh eggs with a medley of Provençale ingredients. Imagine the aroma of ripe tomatoes, fragrant garlic, aromatic herbs, and olives infusing each delicate fold of this savory omelette. Served with a touch of grated cheese and a sprinkle of fresh herbs, this dish transports your tastebuds to the picturesque countryside of Provence, delivering a simple yet exquisite breakfast or brunch experience. Indulge in the timeless charm of French cuisine with Omelette à la Provençale.

Ingredients

- 4 large eggs
- 1 tablespoon olive oil|
- 1/2 cup diced tomatoes
- 1/4 cup diced onion
- 1/4 cup diced bell peppers (red, green, or yellow)
- 2 cloves garlic, minced
- 2 tablespoons chopped fresh basil
- 2 tablespoons chopped fresh parsley
- Salt and pepper to taste
- Grated cheese (optional)

Instructions

1. In a bowl, whisk the eggs until well beaten. Season with salt and pepper according to your taste preferences.

2. Heat olive oil in a non-stick skillet over medium heat. Add the diced onions and sauté until they become translucent.

3. Add the diced tomatoes, bell peppers, and minced garlic to the skillet. Sauté for about 3-4 minutes until the vegetables are slightly softened.

4. Pour the beaten eggs evenly over the sautéed vegetables in the skillet. Allow the eggs to set for a minute or so.

5. Gently lift the edges of the omelette with a spatula, tilting the skillet to let the uncooked eggs flow to the edges and cook.

6. When the eggs are mostly set but still slightly runny on top, sprinkle the chopped basil and parsley over one-half of the omelette.

7. If desired, sprinkle some grated cheese over the herbs. Then, carefully fold the other half of the omelette over the herb-and-cheese side.

8. Let the omelette cook for another minute or until the eggs are fully cooked and the cheese is melted if used.

9. Slide the Omelette à la Provençale onto a plate and serve hot, garnished with extra herbs if desired.

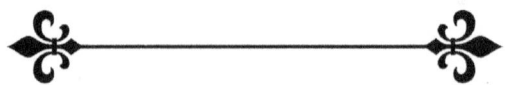

Pain Perdu with Berries

Also known as Lost Bread or French Toast, this classic dish transforms humble ingredients into a decadent and indulgent breakfast or brunch delight. Imagine thick slices of day-old bread soaking up a rich custard, kissed with vanilla and cinnamon. Pan-fried to golden perfection and drizzled with maple syrup, each bite of this Pain Perdu promises a symphony of flavors and a nostalgic embrace of warmth.

Ingredients

- 4 slices of stale bread (preferably brioche or French bread)
- 2 large eggs
- 1/2 cup milk
- 1 teaspoon vanilla extract
- 2 tablespoons granulated sugar
- 1/2 teaspoon ground cinnamon
- Butter for frying
- Mixed berries (strawberries, blueberries, raspberries)
- Maple syrup or honey for drizzling
- Powdered sugar for dusting (optional)

Instructions

1. In a shallow dish or bowl, whisk together the eggs, milk, vanilla extract, granulated sugar, and ground cinnamon until well combined. This mixture will serve as the custard for soaking the bread.

2. Dip each slice of stale bread into the egg mixture, ensuring both sides are well coated but not soaked to the point of falling apart.

3. Heat a non-stick skillet or frying pan over medium heat. Add a knob of butter and let it melt and coat the pan.

4. Place the soaked bread slices onto the skillet and cook for about 2-3 minutes on each side or until they turn golden brown and crispy.

5. Once both sides are cooked, remove the Pain Perdu slices from the skillet and place them on a serving plate.

6. Top the Pain Perdu slices generously with mixed berries.

7. Drizzle maple syrup or honey over the berries and Pain Perdu slices.

8. Optionally, dust the Pain Perdu with a sprinkle of powdered sugar for an extra touch of sweetness.

9. Serve the Pain Perdu with Berries while still warm, allowing the flavors to meld together beautifully.

Omelette à la Napoleon

According to historical records, Napoleon's favorite omelettte was straightforward in preparation. Though the exact recipe does not appear in print, the following recipe is authentic in its simplicity and reliance on high-quality ingredients.

Ingredients

- 4 large eggs
- 2 tablespoons clarified butter or high-quality butter
- Salt and pepper to taste
- Herbs (such as chives, parsley, or tarragon) for garnish (optional)

Instructions

1. Crack the eggs into a bowl and whisk them until they are well combined but not overly frothy.

2. Heat a non-stick skillet or omelette pan over medium-low heat.

3. Add the clarified butter to the heated skillet and swirl it around to coat the surface evenly.

4. Pour the beaten eggs into the skillet, tilting it to spread the eggs across the pan's base.

5. Season the eggs with a pinch of salt and a dash of pepper.

6. As the eggs begin to set on the edges, use a spatula to gently push the cooked portions toward the center, tilting the pan to allow the uncooked eggs to flow to the edges.

7. When the omelette is mostly set but still slightly runny on top, fold it in half using the spatula.

8. Let the omelette cook for another 30 seconds to a minute to ensure it's cooked through but still soft and moist inside.

9. Slide the omelette onto a plate and serve it hot.

Oeufs en Cocotte

This elegant and simple dish translates to "eggs in pots" and encapsulates the essence of a cozy French breakfast. Imagine fresh eggs gently baked in individual ramekins, their yolks soft and runny, surrounded by a medley of flavorful ingredients like cream, herbs, and sometimes ham or cheese. This delightful concoction bakes to perfection, resulting in a harmonious blend of textures and rich, savory flavors. Oeufs en Cocotte offers a taste of indulgence wrapped in the warmth of a comforting embrace, inviting you to savor the essence of French culinary tradition in every bite.

Ingredients

- 4 eggs
- 4 tablespoons heavy cream
- 2 tablespoons grated Gruyère cheese (or another cheese of your choice)
- 2 tablespoons chopped fresh herbs (such as chives, parsley, or tarragon)
- Butter for greasing the ramekins
- Salt and pepper to taste
- Optional additions: cooked ham, sautéed mushrooms, cooked spinach, or other preferred ingredients

Instructions

1. Preheat your oven to 350°F (175°C).

2. Grease four ramekins or oven-safe small dishes with butter to prevent sticking.

3. If using additional ingredients like ham, mushrooms, or spinach, distribute them evenly among the greased ramekins.

4. Crack one egg into each ramekin without breaking the yolk.

5. Spoon one tablespoon of heavy cream over each egg.

6. Season with a pinch of salt and pepper to taste over each egg.

7. Sprinkle grated cheese over the eggs and cream in each ramekin.

8. Place the ramekins in a baking dish and add hot water to the dish, creating a water bath (bain-marie) that reaches about halfway up the sides of the ramekins.

9. Carefully transfer the baking dish to the preheated oven.

10. Bake for about 12-15 minutes or until the egg whites are set but the yolks remain slightly runny. Keep an eye on them as the cooking time can vary depending on your oven and the desired consistency of the eggs.

11. Once done, remove the ramekins from the oven and sprinkle chopped fresh herbs over each serving.

12. Serve the Oeufs en Cocotte immediately, accompanied by crusty bread or toasted soldiers for dipping into the creamy, baked eggs.

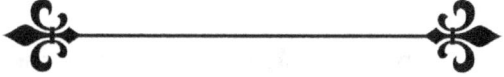

Tartine

Elevate your morning routine with this Tartine recipe, a celebration of simplicity and sophistication in French breakfast culture. A Tartine, in essence, is an open-faced sandwich that transforms humble slices of rustic bread into a canvas for delectable toppings. Picture freshly toasted bread generously adorned with a medley of artisanal spreads, creamy cheeses, ripe avocados, or smoked salmon—each layer a symphony of flavors and textures. This versatile dish offers a customizable and elegant way to start your day, reflecting the timeless charm of French gastronomy.

Ingredients

- Slices of crusty French bread or baguette
- Unsalted butter, softened
- Sliced ham or cured meats (such as prosciutto or salami)
- Sliced cheese (such as Gruyère, Emmental, or Brie)
- Fresh herbs (such as parsley or chives), chopped
- Optional: Dijon mustard or pickles for added flavor

Instructions

1. Toast the slices of French bread or baguette until they're lightly crispy on the edges.

2. Spread a generous layer of softened butter on each slice of toasted bread. This serves as the base for the toppings.

3. Layer the sliced ham or cured meats on top of the buttered bread slices.

4. Place thin slices of cheese on top of the meat layer.

5. If using, spread a small amount of Dijon mustard on the cheese or add some finely chopped pickles for added flavor.

6. Sprinkle the chopped fresh herbs over the Tartines for a burst of freshness.

7. Serve the Tartines immediately, either open-faced or assembled as sandwiches by placing another slice of bread on top, creating a simple yet satisfying meal reminiscent of the flavors prevalent during Napoleon's era.

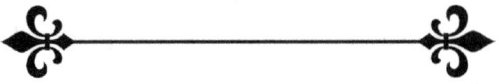

Brioche

During Napoleon's era, brioche was a luxurious and rich bread often enjoyed by the aristocracy. It showcased the simplicity of ingredients and methods prevalent at that time.

Ingredients

- 4 cups all-purpose flour
- 1/2 cup sugar
- 1/2 teaspoon salt
- 1/2 cup milk
- 4-5 large eggs, at room temperature
- 1 1/2 cups unsalted butter, softened
- 1 packet active dry yeast (about 2 1/4 teaspoons)
- Zest of 1 lemon or orange (optional, for flavor)
- Pearl sugar or candied fruits for decoration (optional)

Instructions

1. Warm the milk slightly and dissolve the yeast in it. Let it sit for 5-10 minutes until it becomes frothy.

2. In a large mixing bowl, combine the flour, sugar, and salt. Make a well in the center.

3. Add the frothy yeast mixture and start mixing, gradually incorporating the eggs, one by one, into the flour mixture.

4. Knead the dough until it becomes smooth and elastic. If it's too sticky, you can add a little more flour, but keep in mind that brioche dough tends to be slightly sticky.

5. Slowly add the softened butter, a little at a time, kneading continuously until the butter is fully incorporated and the dough becomes smooth, glossy, and slightly sticky. This can take about 20-30 minutes of kneading by hand.

6. Cover the dough with a clean kitchen towel or plastic wrap and let it rise in a warm place for 2-3 hours, or until it has doubled in size.

7. After the dough has risen, punch it down gently to release the air bubbles. Shape the dough into desired brioche forms: buns, loaves, or a traditional round brioche à tête.

8. Place the shaped dough into greased brioche molds or a baking pan lined with parchment paper.

9. Cover the shaped dough again and let it rise for another 1-2 hours, or until it has doubled in size.

10. Preheat the oven to 375°F (190°C).

11. Optionally, before baking, you can brush the top of the brioche with an egg wash and decorate with pearl sugar or candied fruits.

12. Bake the brioche in the preheated oven for 20-25 minutes (depending on size) or until the top is golden brown and the bread sounds hollow when tapped on the bottom. Let the brioche cool on a wire rack before slicing and serving.

Further Reading:
Chevallier, Jim. *Before the Baguette: The History of French Bread*. Amazon Publishing, 2019.

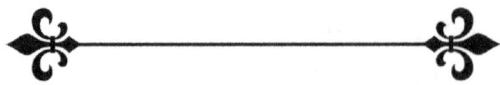

Café au Lait &

Hot Chocolate à la Française

Beverages played a vital role in complementing morning dishes. Café au Lait, a comforting blend of coffee and hot milk, was a staple across all classes. Hot Chocolate à la Française, made with rich, melted chocolate and steamed milk, catered to those with a penchant for decadence in the early morning hours.

Café au Lait

Ingredients

- 1 cup brewed strong coffee
- 1 cup hot milk
- Sugar (optional, to taste)

Instructions

1. Brew a strong cup of coffee using your preferred method, such as a French press or espresso machine.

2. In a saucepan, heat the milk until it's hot but not boiling. You can do this on the stovetop or in the microwave.

3. Pour an equal amount of brewed coffee and hot milk into a large mug.

4. If desired, add sugar to taste and stir until dissolved.

5. Serve the Café au Lait hot and enjoy its smooth and creamy taste, balancing the richness of coffee with the comforting warmth of steamed milk.

Hot Chocolate à la Française

Ingredients

- 2 cups whole milk
- 4 ounces dark chocolate, chopped
- 2 tablespoons granulated sugar (adjust to taste)
- 1/2 teaspoon vanilla extract (optional)
- Whipped cream for topping (optional)
- Cocoa powder or chocolate shavings for garnish (optional)

Instructions

1. In a saucepan, heat the milk over medium-low heat until it's warm, but not boiling.

2. Add the chopped dark chocolate to the warm milk, stirring constantly until the chocolate is completely melted and the mixture is smooth.

3. Stir in the granulated sugar and vanilla extract if using. Adjust sweetness to your preference.

4. Continue to heat the hot chocolate, stirring occasionally, until it reaches your desired drinking temperature.

5. Once ready, pour the Hot Chocolate into mugs.

6. Optionally, top the Hot Chocolate with whipped cream and sprinkle cocoa powder or chocolate shavings for a decorative touch.

7. Serve the Hot Chocolate à la Française while it's hot, savoring its rich and indulgent flavors that harken back to the Napoleonic era's love for decadent treats.

Chapter Five

Savory Beginnings
Appetizers and Starters

A s the sun set on the 18th century, France was not merely a nation but a beacon of culture and refinement. A culinary world of unparalleled sophistication thrived in the illustrious courts of the empire, where power, luxury, and finesse intertwined. Amidst the grandeur and political intrigue of the era, one aspect stood as a testament to the exquisite tastes and social intricacies: the art of appetizers and starters.

In Napoleonic France, the culinary landscape reflected societal norms, hierarchical distinctions, and evolving tastes. The epicurean culture of the era was not solely about satisfying hunger. It was a complex interplay of social hierarchy, evolving tastes, and the art of presentation. Appetizers and starters, though seemingly simple in their role, held a profound significance in the intricate tapestry of Napoleonic dining—a symbol of sophistication, class, and the art of conviviality. Understanding this cultural backdrop provides a deeper appreciation for the culinary expressions that graced the tables of this iconic period.

The divergence of dining experiences among different classes reflected a sharp societal stratification. The elite indulged in extravagant multicourse meals with intricate starters, while the lower classes relied on more straightforward fare for sustenance. Appetizers were not just culinary offerings but social catalysts, setting the tone for a meal and initiating conversations. They were integral in fostering hospitality and signaling the commencement of a formal dining affair.

Appetizers symbolized the host's sophistication and culinary knowledge, reflecting their ability to procure exotic ingredients and present them in refined ways. The selection and presentation were strategic and intended to impress and elevate the dining experience. The display was a focal point, with appetizers arranged in aesthetically pleasing compositions that showcased their beauty and craftsmanship. Appetizers served as conversation starters, allowing guests to engage in discussions while savoring the intricacies of the dishes. Sharing hors d'oeuvres fostered social interaction and created a convivial atmosphere before the formal commencement of the meal.

Pâté de Foie Gras en Croûte

This exquisite dish is a true embodiment of French culinary opulence, featuring velvety foie gras encased in a delicate pastry shell. Enhanced by a carefully crafted blend of spices and seasonings, and enveloped in a golden, flaky crust, this Pâté de Foie Gras en Croûte is a masterpiece of elegance and indulgence. Whether served as a centerpiece or a sophisticated appetizer, this recipe offers a taste of the refined artistry that defines French cuisine.

Ingredients

- 500g fresh foie gras (goose or duck liver)
- 1 teaspoon salt
- 1/2 teaspoon freshly ground black pepper
- 1/4 teaspoon ground nutmeg
- 2 tablespoons cognac or brandy
- 1 sheet puff pastry, thawed if frozen
- 1 egg, beaten (for egg wash)

Instructions

1. Prepare the Foie Gras

- Clean the foie gras, removing any veins or membranes. Season it with salt, pepper, and nutmeg. Gently pour the cognac or brandy over the seasoned foie gras and let it marinate for at least 2 hours, preferably overnight, in the refrigerator.

2. Roll Out the Puff Pastry

- Preheat your oven to 400°F (200°C).
- On a lightly floured surface, roll out the puff pastry into a rectangle large enough to wrap the foie gras completely.

3. Wrap the Foie Gras

- Place the marinated foie gras in the center of the puff pastry. Fold the pastry over the foie gras to completely encase it, ensuring there are no openings or gaps. Seal the edges by pressing them together.

4. Decorate and Vent the Pâté

- Use any excess pastry to create decorative shapes or patterns on the top of the pâté. Use a knife to create a few small slits on the top to allow steam to escape during baking.

5. Brush with Egg Wash

- Brush the entire surface of the pastry with the beaten egg. This will give the pâté a beautiful golden color when baked.

6. Bake the Pâté

- Place the prepared pâté on a baking sheet lined with parchment paper. Bake in the preheated oven for about 25-30 minutes, or until the pastry is golden brown and crispy.

7. Chill and Serve

- Once baked, allow the pâté to cool to room temperature. For the best flavor, refrigerate it for at least 24 hours before serving. Serve thin slices of the pâté on toasted bread or crackers as an elegant appetizer.

Truffled Mushroom Vol-au-Vent

This Truffled Mushroom Vol-au-Vent offers a contemporary twist on a classic dish. It combines the earthy richness of mushrooms with the luxurious essence of truffle oil, all encased in delicate and flaky puff pastry. It makes for an impressive appetizer fit for special occasions or elegant gatherings.

Ingredients

- 2 sheets puff pastry, thawed if frozen
- 500g mixed mushrooms (such as cremini, shiitake, and oyster), finely chopped
- 2 tablespoons butter
- 2 tablespoons olive oil
- 2 cloves garlic, minced
- 2 shallots, finely chopped
- 2 tablespoons truffle oil
- 1/4 cup heavy cream
- Salt and pepper to taste
- Chopped fresh parsley for garnish
- 1 egg, beaten (for egg wash)

Instructions

1. Prepare the Puff Pastry

- Preheat your oven to 400°F (200°C). Cut the puff pastry sheets into squares or rounds slightly larger than the size of your desired vol-au-vent shape. Using a smaller cutter, create a smaller shape within each piece to form the pastry lids. Place the larger pieces on a baking sheet lined with parchment paper.

2. Bake the Puff Pastry

- Brush the smaller shapes with the beaten egg (this will act as a glue). Place the smaller shapes on top of the larger ones to create a raised border. Brush the entire pastry with egg wash.

- Bake in the preheated oven for about 15-20 minutes or until golden brown and puffed. Remove and set aside.

3. Prepare the Mushroom Filling

- In a large skillet, heat the butter and olive oil over medium heat. Add the minced garlic and shallots, sautéing until softened and fragrant.
- Add the chopped mushrooms to the skillet and cook until they release their moisture and start to brown, about 8-10 minutes.
- Pour in the truffle oil and heavy cream, stirring to combine. Let it simmer gently for another 5 minutes until the cream has slightly thickened. Season with salt and pepper to taste.

4. Assemble the Vol-au-Vent

- Carefully remove the top of each baked puff pastry to create a lid. Fill the hollowed-out centers with the truffled mushroom mixture.

5. Garnish and Serve

- Garnish each vol-au-vent with chopped fresh parsley for a pop of color and added flavor. Place the pastry lids on top at a slight angle to showcase the filling. Serve warm.

Oysters à la Talleyrand

This dish is a tribute to the sophistication and taste for fine dining attributed to renowned French diplomat Charles Maurice de Talleyrand-Périgord. The specifics of this dish vary, but it typically involves serving oysters in a rich sauce. The creamy sauce complements the briny flavor of the oysters, creating a luxurious and indulgent culinary experience reminiscent of the opulent dining tables of the Napoleonic era.

Ingredients

- 12 fresh oysters, shucked and on the half-shell
- 4 tablespoons unsalted butter
- 2 shallots, finely chopped
- 1/4 cup dry white wine
- 1/2 cup heavy cream
- 1 tablespoon fresh parsley, finely chopped
- 1 tablespoon fresh chives, finely chopped
- Salt and white pepper to taste
- Lemon wedges for garnish

Instructions

1. Prepare the Oysters

- Preheat your oven to 450°F (230°C).
- Arrange the shucked oysters on a baking sheet or oven-safe dish filled with rock salt to stabilize them.

2. Prepare the Sauce

- In a saucepan over medium heat, melt the butter. Add the finely chopped shallots and sauté until translucent.

3. Deglaze with White Wine

- Pour the dry white wine into the saucepan, stirring gently to deglaze the pan and incorporate the flavors. Allow it to simmer for a couple of minutes until the alcohol evaporates.

4. Add Cream and Herbs

- Pour in the heavy cream, stirring continuously. Add the finely chopped parsley and chives. Season the sauce with salt and white pepper to taste. Let the sauce simmer for a few minutes until it thickens slightly.

5. Cook the Oysters

- Place the baking sheet with the oysters in the preheated oven for about 5 minutes or until the oysters' edges begin to curl.

6. Finish the Dish

- Remove the oysters from the oven. Spoon a generous amount of the prepared sauce over each oyster.

7. Garnish and Serve

- Garnish the Oysters à la Talleyrand with a sprinkle of fresh herbs and serve with lemon wedges for an added touch of freshness.
- Place the oysters back into the oven for an additional 2-3 minutes to heat the sauce. Remove and serve immediately.

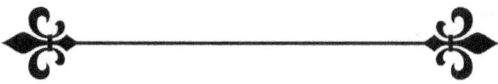

Consommé Malmaison

This consommé typically includes a variety of finely diced vegetables and small meatballs or quenelles. It is a classic French clear soup named after the Château de Malmaison, a residence of Napoleon Bonaparte and Empress Joséphine.

Ingredients

For the Consommé Base

- 8 cups beef consommé or homemade beef broth
- 1/2 cup carrots, finely diced
- 1/2 cup celery, finely diced
- 1/2 cup leeks, finely diced
- 1/4 cup onion, finely diced
- 2 cloves garlic, minced
- 1 bouquet garni (a bundle of fresh herbs like thyme, parsley, and bay leaf tied together)
- Salt and pepper to taste

For the Meatballs

- 1/2 lb ground beef or veal
- 1 egg
- 2 tablespoons breadcrumbs
- 1 tablespoon finely chopped parsley
- Salt and pepper to taste

Instructions

1. Prepare the Consommé Base

- In a large pot, bring the beef consommé or beef broth to a gentle simmer over medium heat. Add the finely diced carrots, celery, leeks, onion, minced garlic, and the bouquet garni to the pot.

2. Simmer the Consommé

- Let the consommé and vegetables simmer gently for about 20-25 minutes until the vegetables are tender and have imparted their flavors into the broth. Skim off any foam or impurities that rise to the surface.

3. Prepare the Meatballs

- In a mixing bowl, combine the ground beef or veal with the egg, breadcrumbs, finely chopped parsley, salt, and pepper. Mix until well combined.
- Form small meatballs (about 1-inch in diameter) with the meat mixture.

4. Cook the Meatballs

- Gently drop the meatballs into the simmering consommé. Let them cook for about 10-15 minutes until they are cooked through and tender.

5. Remove Bouquet Garni, Adjust Seasoning and Serve

- Remove the pot from the heat and discard the bouquet garni. Taste the consommé and adjust the seasoning with salt and pepper if needed.
- Ladle the clear consommé with the vegetables and meatballs into serving bowls. Ensure each bowl has a portion of the vegetables and a few meatballs. Serve hot.

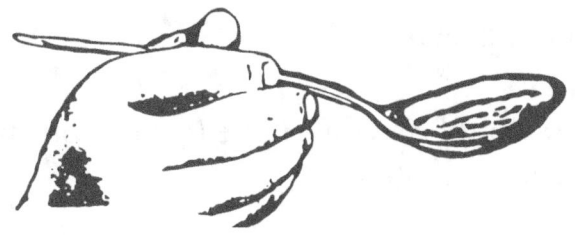

Consommé Madrilène

Consommé Madrilène is a classic soup that combines the richness of beef consommé with the vibrant flavors of tomato and aromatic vegetables.

Ingredients

- 8 cups beef consommé or homemade beef broth
- 2 cups tomato purée
- 1/2 cup carrots, finely diced
- 1/2 cup celery, finely diced
- 1/2 cup onion, finely diced
- 2 cloves garlic, minced
- 1 bouquet garni (a bundle of fresh herbs like thyme, parsley, and bay leaf tied together)
- Salt and pepper to taste
- Olive oil for sautéing

Instructions

1. Prepare the Vegetables

- In a soup pot or large saucepan, heat a little olive oil over medium heat. Add the finely diced carrots, celery, onion, and minced garlic. Sauté until the vegetables are tender and aromatic.

2. Add Tomato Purée and Consommé

- Pour in the tomato purée and beef consommé (or beef broth) into the pot with the sautéed vegetables. Stir well to combine.

3. Simmer with Bouquet Garni

- Add the bouquet garni (herb bundle) to the pot. Bring the mixture to a gentle simmer over medium-low heat. Let it simmer for about 30-40 minutes, allowing the flavors to meld and the vegetables to infuse the soup.

4. Remove Bouquet Garni and Season

- Once the soup has simmered and the flavors have developed, remove the bouquet garni from the pot. Taste the consommé and adjust the seasoning with salt and pepper according to your preference.

5. Strain the Consommé:

- To achieve a clear consommé, carefully strain the soup through a fine-mesh sieve or cheesecloth to remove the solids, leaving a clear and flavorful broth.

6. Garnish and Serve

- Optionally, you can garnish each bowl with a sprig of fresh parsley or a drizzle of olive oil before serving for added flavor and presentation.
- Ladle the clear Consommé Madrilène into serving bowls. Serve hot.

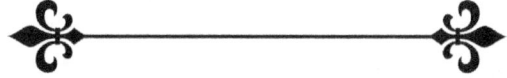

Consommé Celestine

Consommé Celestine, with its delicate egg-enriched puff pastry squares floating in flavorful, clear broth, presents an elegant and delightful experience.

Ingredients

For the Consommé

- 8 cups beef consommé or homemade beef broth
- 1/2 cup carrots, finely diced
- 1/2 cup celery, finely diced
- 1/2 cup onion, finely diced

- 2 cloves garlic, minced
- 1 bouquet garni (a bundle of fresh herbs like thyme, parsley, and bay leaf tied together)
- Salt and pepper to taste
- Olive oil for sautéing

For the Celestine

- 4 eggs
- 2 tablespoons milk
- Salt and pepper to taste
- 4 sheets of puff pastry, thawed if frozen

Instructions

1. Prepare the Vegetables

- In a soup pot or large saucepan, heat a little olive oil over medium heat. Add the finely diced carrots, celery, onion, and minced garlic. Sauté until the vegetables are tender and aromatic.

2. Prepare the Consommé Base

- Pour the beef consommé (or beef broth) into the pot with the sautéed vegetables. Stir well to combine.

3. Simmer with Bouquet Garni

- Add the bouquet garni (herb bundle) to the pot. Bring the mixture to a gentle simmer over medium-low heat. Let it simmer for about 30-40 minutes to allow the flavors to meld.

4. Strain the Consommé

- Once the soup has simmered and the flavors have developed, remove the pot from heat. Carefully strain the soup through a fine-mesh sieve or cheesecloth to remove the solids, leaving a clear and flavorful broth.

5. Prepare the Celestine

- Preheat your oven to the temperature recommended on the puff pastry package.
- In a bowl, beat the eggs with milk, salt, and pepper to create an egg wash.
- Lay out the puff pastry sheets and cut them into small squares or rectangles.
- Brush each puff pastry square with the egg wash and bake them in the preheated oven according to the package instructions until they're golden brown and puffed.

6. Serve the Consommé and Add Celestine

- Ladle the clear Consommé Celestine into serving bowls.
- Place a few of the baked puff pastry squares (Celestine) in each bowl of consommé before serving.

Canapés à la Régence

Canapés à la Régence celebrate elegance and sophistication with refined ingredients atop crispy bases. These appetizers delight guests with their harmonious blend of flavors and textures, making them a splendid addition to any gathering.

Ingredients

Base

- Slices of baguette or small squares of toasted brioche or puff pastry

Toppings (Mix and Match)

- Smoked salmon or trout
- Foie gras mousse or pâté
- Truffle slices or truffle-infused elements (e.g., truffle oil)
- Caviar or salmon roe
- Herbed cream cheese or crème fraîche
- Thinly sliced prosciutto or cured meats
- Fresh herbs like dill, chives, or parsley for garnish
- Pickled vegetables (capers, cornichons, or pickled onions) for tang and texture

Instructions

1. Prepare the Base

- Slice the baguette into thin rounds or cut the brioche or puff pastry into small squares. Toast or bake them until they're golden and crisp.

2. Prepare the Toppings

- Arrange an assortment of toppings based on your preference and availability. For example:
- For a classic touch, spread a layer of foie gras mousse or pâté on the base.
- Top another set of bases with herbed cream cheese or crème fraîche.
- Place thin slices of smoked salmon or trout on some bases.
- Add a dollop of caviar or salmon roe atop certain canapés.
- Arrange slices of truffle or drizzle truffle oil on a few.

3. Assemble the Canapés

- Once the bases are prepared and toppings are arranged, delicately assemble the canapés. You can mix and match the toppings or create uniform canapés based on individual preferences.

4. Garnish and Serve

- Garnish the canapés with fresh herbs like dill, chives, or parsley for a decorative touch. You can also add a small pickled vegetable on top for an extra burst of flavor and texture.

Escargot à la Bourguignonne

This dish is an authentic French delicacy, offering a rich herb-infused buttery experience that complements escargot's unique taste and texture.

Ingredients

- 24 canned escargot shells
- 24 canned escargot (or snails), rinsed and drained
- 1/2 cup unsalted butter, softened
- 4 cloves garlic, minced
- 2 tablespoons fresh parsley, finely chopped
- 1 tablespoon shallots, finely chopped
- 1 teaspoon fresh thyme, chopped
- 1 teaspoon fresh rosemary, chopped
- 1 teaspoon lemon juice
- Salt and black pepper to taste
- Baguette or French bread, for serving

Instructions

1. Prepare the Garlic Herb Butter

- In a mixing bowl, combine the softened butter, minced garlic, chopped parsley, shallots, thyme, rosemary, lemon juice, salt, and black pepper. Mix thoroughly until all ingredients are well incorporated into the butter.

2. Prepare the Escargot Shells

- Rinse and dry the escargot shells thoroughly. Place one escargot into each shell.

3. Fill the Shells with Garlic Herb Butter

- Spoon the prepared garlic herb butter generously into each escargot shell, covering the snail completely with the butter mixture.

4. Bake the Escargot

- Preheat your oven to 400°F (200°C). Arrange the filled escargot shells in a snail plate or a baking dish.
- Bake in the preheated oven for approximately 10-12 minutes or until the butter is sizzling and bubbling.

5. Serve

- Remove the escargot from the oven. Traditionally, escargot à la Bourguignonne is served hot and sizzling. Place the escargot plate on a larger plate to avoid direct contact with the table's surface.
- Accompany the escargot with slices of baguette or French bread to soak up the flavorful garlic herb butter.

Chapter Six

Victorious Victuals
Main Dishes and Entrées

F rom the bustling kitchens of Parisian palaces to the humble hearths of rural homes, the significance of main courses and entrees extended far beyond mere nourishment. They were the centerpieces of communal gatherings, the tools of culinary diplomacy, and the expressions of a nation's identity. In the early 19th century, France stood at the crossroads of revolution, war, and cultural renaissance. This era was when the art of cuisine transformed as dynamically as the political landscape. The culinary stage of Napoleonic France showcased tradition, innovation, and social hierarchy.

Main courses showcased culinary excellence, where tastes, techniques, and presentation converged to create dishes fit for royalty. They were not merely meals but experiences. They were an amalgamation of meticulous preparation, gastronomic mastery, and a celebration of the finest ingredients. The preparation of these entrees involved many methods—from slow braising to precise seasoning—each step aimed at elevating the innate flavors.

The dining table was more than a place to satiate hunger. It was a theater for societal norms and stratification. In the grand halls of the nobility, meals were elaborate, multi-course affairs that showcased opulence through extravagant ingredients and meticulous presentations. Each dish was a statement, an emblem of wealth and status. Conversely, in the homes of the commoners, repasts were simpler, relying on locally available produce and recipes passed down through generations, forming the backbone of everyday cooking. Dishes showcased the region's agricultural bounty through locally available ingredients. Stews, soups, and one-pot meals were commonplace, utilizing humble components like root vegetables, grains, and inexpensive cuts of meat.

Coq au Vin

This rustic yet refined chicken dish braised in red wine, aromatics, and mushrooms was a staple at Napoleon Bonaparte's table—a testament to his appreciation for provincial France's hearty and comforting flavor. Napoleon developed a fondness for this dish's rustic charm and robust flavors while traversing the French countryside during his campaigns, adapting it to suit his palate. Its preparation mirrored the resilience and resourcefulness of the French countryside, elements that resonated with the emperor's strategic prowess on the battlefield.

Ingredients

- 1 whole chicken (about 3-4 pounds), cut into pieces
- 4 slices of bacon, chopped
- 2 tablespoons butter
- 1 onion, finely chopped
- 3 cloves garlic, minced
- 2 carrots, peeled and sliced
- 10-12 pearl onions, peeled
- 8 ounces button mushrooms, halved or quartered
- 2 tablespoons all-purpose flour
- 2 cups red wine (such as Burgundy)
- 1 cup chicken broth
- 2-3 sprigs fresh thyme
- 2 bay leaves
- Salt and pepper to taste
- Chopped fresh parsley for garnish

Instructions

1. Season the chicken pieces with salt and pepper. In a large Dutch oven or heavy-bottomed pot, cook the chopped bacon over medium heat until crispy. Remove the bacon with a slotted spoon and set it aside.

2. In the same pot with the bacon fat, add 1 tablespoon of butter. Brown the chicken pieces in batches, about 5-6 minutes per side. Remove the chicken and set it aside.

3. Add the remaining tablespoon of butter to the pot. Sauté the chopped onion, garlic, carrots, pearl onions, and mushrooms until they start to soften, about 5-6 minutes.

4. Sprinkle the vegetables with flour and stir to coat. Cook for another 1-2 minutes to cook out the raw flour taste.

5. Pour in the red wine and chicken broth, stirring to deglaze the pot, and scrape up any browned bits from the bottom. Add the chicken pieces back into the pot along with the crispy bacon, thyme sprigs, and bay leaves.

6. Bring the mixture to a simmer, then reduce the heat to low. Cover the pot and let it gently simmer for 1 to 1 1/2 hours, or until the chicken is tender and cooked through.

7. Once done, remove the chicken pieces and set them aside. Simmer the sauce uncovered for an additional 10-15 minutes to thicken slightly.

8. Taste the sauce and adjust the seasoning if needed. Remove the thyme sprigs and bay leaves.

9. To serve, place the chicken pieces on a serving platter and spoon the vegetables and sauce over the top. Garnish with chopped fresh parsley.

Enjoy your Coq au Vin with crusty bread, mashed potatoes, or over a bed of cooked egg noodles. The flavors deepen if you prepare this dish a day ahead and reheat it before serving.

Beef Bourguignon

In the heart of Burgundy, amidst rolling vineyards and picturesque landscapes, emerged a dish that epitomized the soul of French countryside cuisine—Beef Bourguignon. This rich and sumptuous stew of beef braised in red wine, infused with aromatic herbs and vegetables, found its way onto Napoleon's table, earning a cherished place among his favored culinary indulgences. Legend has it that Napoleon, drawn to its earthy and comforting essence, often sought solace in the warm embrace of this dish, especially during times when the rigors of leadership weighed heavily upon him.

Ingredients

- 2 1/2 to 3 pounds beef chuck, cut into chunks (around 2-inch pieces)
- 4 slices of bacon, chopped
- 2 tablespoons olive oil
- 1 onion, finely chopped
- 3 cloves garlic, minced
- 2 carrots, peeled and sliced
- 2 stalks celery, sliced
- 2 tablespoons all-purpose flour
- 2 cups red wine (Burgundy or any full-bodied red)
- 2 cups beef broth
- 2 tablespoons tomato paste
- 1 tablespoon fresh thyme leaves
- 2 bay leaves
- Salt and pepper to taste
- 1 pound mushrooms, quartered
- Chopped fresh parsley for garnish

Instructions

1. Preheat your oven to 325°F (165°C).

2. In a large Dutch oven or heavy-bottomed pot, cook the chopped bacon over medium heat until it becomes crispy. Remove the bacon with a slotted spoon and set it aside.

3. In the same pot with the bacon fat, add the olive oil. Brown the beef chunks in batches, about 5-6 minutes per batch. Remove the beef and set it aside.

4. Add the chopped onion, garlic, carrots, and celery to the pot. Cook, stirring occasionally, for about 5-6 minutes until they begin to soften.

5. Sprinkle the vegetables with flour and stir well to coat. Cook for another minute or so to cook out the raw flour taste.

6. Pour in the red wine and beef broth, stirring to deglaze the pot, and scrape up any browned bits from the bottom. Add the tomato paste, thyme leaves, bay leaves, and the cooked beef and bacon back into the pot.

7. Bring the mixture to a simmer, then cover the pot and transfer it to the preheated oven. Let it bake for about 2 to 2 1/2 hours, or until the beef becomes fork-tender.

8. About 30 minutes before the beef is done, heat a skillet over medium heat and add a little oil. Sauté the mushrooms until they are browned and tender. Season them lightly with salt and pepper.

9. Once the beef is done, remove the pot from the oven. Stir in the sautéed mushrooms into the stew.

10. Taste and adjust seasoning with salt and pepper if needed. Remove the bay leaves.

11. Serve the Beef Bourguignon hot, garnished with chopped fresh parsley. It pairs wonderfully with mashed potatoes, crusty bread, or noodles.

This dish improves in flavor if prepared a day in advance and reheated before serving.

Poulet à la Marengo

Poulet à la Marengo is a historical French dish allegedly originating from the Battle of Marengo in 1800, where Napoleon achieved a significant victory. This classic recipe pays homage to that momentous event with a delightful combination of flavors. The dish features sautéed poultry (typically chicken) cooked in a flavorful sauce made from tomatoes, white wine, and a medley of aromatic herbs such as garlic, thyme, and bay leaves. Poulet à la Marengo is a celebration of the bounties of the French countryside and stands as a delicious reminder of history.

Ingredients

- 1 whole chicken (about 3-4 pounds), cut into pieces
- Salt and freshly ground black pepper
- 1/4 cup all-purpose flour, for dredging
- 4 tablespoons unsalted butter
- 2 tablespoons olive oil
- 1 onion, finely chopped
- 2 cloves garlic, minced
- 1 red bell pepper, diced
- 1 can (14 ounces) crushed tomatoes
- 1/2 cup chicken broth
- 1/2 cup dry white wine
- 1 teaspoon tomato paste
- 1 teaspoon chopped fresh thyme
- 1 bay leaf
- 1 cup button mushrooms, quartered
- 1/2 cup black or green olives, pitted
- Chopped fresh parsley for garnish

Instructions

1. Season the chicken pieces generously with salt and pepper. Dredge the chicken in flour, shaking off any excess.

2. In a large skillet or Dutch oven, heat 2 tablespoons of butter and 1 tablespoon of olive oil over medium-high heat. Add the chicken pieces and cook until they turn golden brown on all sides, about 5-6 minutes. Remove the chicken from the skillet and set it aside.

3. In the same skillet, add the remaining butter and olive oil. Sauté the chopped onion, garlic, and diced bell pepper until they start to soften, about 4-5 minutes.

4. Stir in the crushed tomatoes, chicken broth, white wine, tomato paste, thyme, and bay leaf. Bring the mixture to a simmer.

5. Return the browned chicken pieces to the skillet, along with any accumulated juices. Cover the skillet and simmer gently over low heat for about 30-35 minutes, or until the chicken is cooked through and tender.

6. In the last 10 minutes of cooking, add the quartered mushrooms and olives to the skillet, stirring gently to combine. Allow the flavors to meld together.

7. Once the chicken is fully cooked and the sauce has thickened slightly, taste and adjust seasoning if needed. Remove the bay leaf.

8. Serve the Poulet à la Marengo hot, garnished with chopped fresh parsley. Rice, pasta, or crusty bread are good accompaniments to soaking up the flavorful sauce.

Further Reading:
Uffindell, Andrew. *Napoleon's Chicken Marengo*. Havertown, PA: Casemate Publishers, 2011.

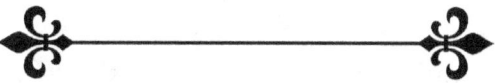

Lobster Thermidor

A dish that graced the tables of the elite, Lobster Thermidor exuded luxury and extravagance. Succulent lobster meat cooked in a creamy, brandy-infused sauce, topped with a gratin of cheese and breadcrumbs, presented a symphony of flavors and textures fit for nobility. It is a culinary masterpiece that captivates the senses with its exquisite flavors and elegant presentation, making it a time-honored choice for special occasions and fine dining experiences.

Ingredients

- 2 cooked lobsters (about 1 1/2 pounds each)
- 4 tablespoons unsalted butter
- 2 tablespoons all-purpose flour
- 1 cup whole milk
- 1/2 cup heavy cream
- 1/4 cup grated Gruyere or Parmesan cheese
- 2 tablespoons dry white wine
- 1 tablespoon Dijon mustard
- 2 tablespoons chopped fresh parsley
- Salt and freshly ground black pepper, to taste
- Pinch of cayenne pepper (optional)
- Lemon wedges, for serving
- Extra parsley for garnish

Instructions

1. Preheat your oven to 375°F (190°C).

2. Prepare the lobsters by removing the meat from the shells. Crack the shells and carefully remove the meat, chopping it into bite-sized pieces. Set aside the empty lobster shells for later use as serving vessels.

3. In a saucepan, melt 2 tablespoons of butter over medium heat. Add the flour and whisk continuously for about 2 minutes to create a roux.

4. Gradually pour in the milk and heavy cream while whisking constantly to avoid lumps. Cook the sauce until it thickens and coats the back of a spoon, about 5-7 minutes.

5. Stir in the grated cheese, white wine, Dijon mustard, chopped parsley, salt, black pepper, and a pinch of cayenne pepper (if using). Continue to cook for another 2-3 minutes until the cheese melts and the sauce is smooth and creamy.

6. In a separate pan, melt the remaining 2 tablespoons of butter over medium heat. Add the chopped lobster meat and sauté briefly, about 1-2 minutes, just until heated through.

7. Add the sautéed lobster meat to the creamy sauce, stirring gently to coat the lobster evenly.

8. Arrange the empty lobster shells on a baking dish or oven-safe serving tray. Spoon the lobster mixture into the shells, filling them generously.

9. Place the filled lobster shells in the preheated oven and bake for about 10-15 minutes, or until the tops are golden brown and bubbly.

10. Remove the Lobster Thermidor from the oven. Garnish with additional chopped parsley and serve immediately with lemon wedges on the side.

Sole Meunière

This beloved recipe features delicate sole fillets dredged in flour and pan-fried to golden perfection in a meunière sauce. The sauce blends browned butter, lemon juice, and chopped parsley, creating a symphony of flavors that perfectly complements this tender fish. The preparation is uncomplicated, allowing the fish's natural flavors to shine.

Ingredients

- 4 sole fillets (about 6-8 ounces each), skinless
- Salt and freshly ground black pepper
- All-purpose flour, for dredging
- 4 tablespoons unsalted butter
- 2 tablespoons olive oil
- 1-2 tablespoons freshly squeezed lemon juice
- 2 tablespoons chopped fresh parsley
- Lemon wedges, for serving

Instructions

1. Pat the sole fillets dry with paper towels. Season them lightly with salt and pepper on both sides.

2. Dredge the seasoned fillets in flour, shaking off any excess. This helps create a light coating for the fish.

3. In a large skillet, heat 2 tablespoons of butter and 1 tablespoon of olive oil over medium-high heat until the butter begins to foam but doesn't brown.

4. Gently place the floured sole fillets in the skillet, being careful not to overcrowd the pan. Cook the fillets for about 2-3 minutes on each side, or until they turn golden brown and are cooked through. (You may need to cook them in batches if your skillet is not large enough.)

5. As the sole fillets cook, transfer them to a serving platter or individual plates.

6. Once all the fillets are cooked, wipe the skillet clean with paper towels. This step helps ensure that the brown butter sauce doesn't get burnt.

7. In the cleaned skillet, melt the remaining 2 tablespoons of butter over medium heat. Allow the butter to foam and turn a golden brown color while swirling the skillet occasionally. Be careful not to let it burn.

8. Once the butter turns a rich golden brown and has a nutty aroma, remove the skillet

from the heat. Stir in the freshly squeezed lemon juice and chopped parsley, swirling the skillet to combine.

9. Spoon the brown butter and lemon sauce over the cooked sole fillets.

10. Serve the Sole Meunière immediately, garnished with additional fresh parsley and lemon wedges on the side.

Canard à l'Orange à la Napoleon

Creating a specific recipe for Canard à l'Orange à la Napoleon involves infusing the classic Canard à l'Orange with an element that might represent Napoleon's era. You can do this by incorporating ingredients or techniques that were popular or associated with French cuisine during Napoleon's time.

Ingredients

- 2 duck breasts (about 1 to 1 1/2 pounds total), skin on
- Salt and freshly ground black pepper
- 2 tablespoons olive oil
- 1/2 cup freshly squeezed orange juice
- Zest of 1 orange
- 1/4 cup chicken broth
- 2 tablespoons red wine vinegar
- 2 tablespoons honey
- 2 tablespoons unsalted butter
- 1 tablespoon Cognac or Brandy (reminiscent of the era's spirits)
- A pinch of ground cloves or a few whole cloves (a common spice in the Napoleonic era)
- Orange slices for garnish
- Chopped fresh parsley for garnish

Instructions

1. Preheat your oven to 400°F (200°C).

2. Score the skin of the duck breasts in a crisscross pattern without cutting into the meat. Season the duck breasts generously with salt and pepper on both sides.

3. Heat a skillet (preferably oven-safe) over medium-high heat. Add the olive oil to the skillet. Once hot, place the duck breasts skin-side down in the skillet. Sear the duck breasts for about 4-5 minutes, or until the skin turns golden brown and crispy. Flip the breasts and sear the other side for 1-2 minutes.

4. Transfer the skillet to the preheated oven and roast the duck breasts for about 10-12 minutes for medium-rare or until desired doneness. Remove the duck breasts from the skillet and let them rest on a cutting board, tented with foil.

5. While the duck rests, prepare the orange sauce. In the same skillet used for cooking the duck, discard most of the duck fat, leaving about a tablespoon in the skillet.

6. Place the skillet back on the stovetop over medium heat. Add the orange juice, orange zest, chicken broth, red wine vinegar, honey, and a pinch of ground cloves or a few whole cloves. Bring the mixture to a simmer and let it reduce by half, stirring occasionally.

7. Once the sauce has reduced, stir in the butter and Cognac or Brandy until the butter melts and the sauce becomes glossy. Season the sauce with salt and pepper to taste.

8. Slice the rested duck breasts diagonally and arrange them on a serving platter. Drizzle the orange sauce over the duck slices.

9. Garnish with orange slices and chopped fresh parsley.

Canard à la Presse

Canard à la Presse is a traditional French dish utilizing a specialized press to extract juices from a roasted duck. This adapted version recreates the dish's essence without using the traditional press, which may not readily be available. It allows you to enjoy a flavorful roasted duck with a rich sauce derived from its juices.

Ingredients

- 1 whole duck (about 4-5 pounds)
- Salt and freshly ground black pepper
- 2 tablespoons olive oil
- 2 shallots, finely chopped
- 2 cloves garlic, minced
- 1 cup red wine
- 1 cup chicken or duck broth
- 2 tablespoons unsalted butter
- 1 tablespoon all-purpose flour (optional, for thickening)
- A pinch of dried thyme
- A pinch of dried rosemary
- Fresh parsley for garnish

Instructions

1. Preheat your oven to 400°F (200°C).

2. Rinse the duck inside and out, then pat it dry with paper towels. Season the duck generously with salt and pepper, both inside and outside.

3. Heat olive oil in an oven-safe skillet or roasting pan over medium-high heat. Place the seasoned duck in the skillet, breast-side down, and sear it until the skin turns golden brown, about 5-6 minutes. Flip the duck and sear the other side for an additional 2-3 minutes.

4. Transfer the skillet or roasting pan to the preheated oven. Roast the duck for about 60-75 minutes or until the internal temperature reaches 165°F (74°C) and the juices run clear. Remove the duck from the oven and let it rest for 10-15 minutes.

5. While the duck rests, prepare the sauce. In a saucepan, sauté the shallots and garlic in a tablespoon of the duck fat or butter over medium heat until softened.

6. Pour in the red wine and chicken or duck broth. Add a pinch of dried thyme and rosemary. Simmer the sauce over medium heat until it reduces by half, stirring occasionally. If you prefer a thicker sauce, mix in a tablespoon of flour (mixed with a little water) to thicken it.

7. Strain the sauce through a fine-mesh sieve, pressing to extract as much liquid as possible. Return the strained sauce to the saucepan and keep it warm.

8. Carve the roasted duck into serving portions.

9. To serve, place the duck portions on plates and spoon the sauce over the meat. Garnish with fresh parsley.

Poulet en Vessie

Poulet en Vessie, or Chicken in a Bladder, is a traditional French dish that entails cooking a chicken inside a pig's bladder. The technique is quite elaborate and might not be practical for home cooking due to using a bladder. This adapted recipe captures the flavors of Poulet en Vessie by infusing the chicken with aromatics and cooking it in a flavorful broth, reminiscent of the traditional method without using a bladder.

Ingredients

- 1 whole chicken (about 3-4 pounds)
- Salt and freshly ground black pepper
- 4 tablespoons unsalted butter
- 4 shallots, finely chopped
- 2 cloves garlic, minced
- 1 cup white wine
- 1 cup chicken broth
- 2 tablespoons chopped fresh tarragon (or use parsley, thyme, or a combination)
- 1 lemon, sliced
- Kitchen twine or cooking string

Instructions

1. Preheat your oven to 375°F (190°C).

2. Rinse the chicken inside and out, then pat it dry with paper towels. Season the cavity and skin of the chicken generously with salt and pepper.

3. In a large oven-safe skillet or Dutch oven, melt 2 tablespoons of butter over medium-high heat. Place the chicken in the skillet, breast-side down, and sear it until the skin turns golden brown, about 5-6 minutes. Flip the chicken and sear the other side for an additional 2-3 minutes.

4. Remove the chicken from the skillet and set it aside on a plate. Discard any excess fat from the skillet, leaving about a tablespoon.

5. In the same skillet, melt the remaining butter over medium heat. Sauté the shallots and garlic until they turn translucent and aromatic, about 3-4 minutes.

6. Deglaze the skillet with white wine, scraping up any browned bits from the bottom. Let the wine simmer for a couple of minutes to reduce slightly.

7. Pour in the chicken broth and add the chopped tarragon. Return the seared chicken to the skillet, placing lemon slices inside the cavity.

8. Tie the legs of the chicken together with kitchen twine to keep the shape intact. Cover

the skillet with a lid or aluminum foil.

9. Transfer the skillet to the preheated oven and roast the chicken for about 60-75 minutes or until the internal temperature reaches 165°F (74°C) and the juices run clear. Baste the chicken with the pan juices occasionally during cooking.

10. Remove the chicken from the oven and let it rest for 10-15 minutes before carving.

11. Serve the Poulet en Vessie-style chicken hot, garnished with additional fresh herbs if desired.

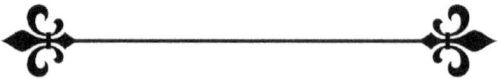

Pot-au-Feu

Pot-au-Feu, a quintessential French dish, translates into "pot on the fire," capturing the essence of its humble origins. This simple, traditional, comforting stew showcases the hearty flavors of slowly simmered meats and vegetables. Typically prepared in a large pot, pot-au-feu features a mix of beef cuts, such as brisket, short ribs, and marrow bones, cooked with various root vegetables like carrots, turnips, and leeks.

Ingredients

- 2 pounds beef chuck roast, cut into large chunks
- 1 pound beef marrow bones (optional)
- 2 onions, peeled and left whole
- 4 carrots, peeled and left whole
- 4 celery stalks, left whole
- 2 leeks, cleaned and left whole
- 4 cloves garlic, peeled
- 1 bouquet garni (a bundle of herbs like thyme, parsley, and bay leaves, tied together)
- Salt and freshly ground black pepper
- 8-10 cups beef broth or water (enough to cover the ingredients)
- 4-6 small potatoes, peeled (optional)

- Dijon mustard, for serving
- Crusty bread, for serving
- Chopped fresh parsley for garnish

Instructions

1. In a large stockpot, place the beef chunks, beef marrow bones (if using), whole onions, carrots, celery, leeks, garlic cloves, and bouquet garni. Season generously with salt and pepper.

2. Pour enough beef broth or water into the pot to cover all the ingredients.

3. Bring the pot to a gentle boil over medium-high heat. Skim off any foam that rises to the surface.

4. Reduce the heat to low, cover the pot partially with a lid, and let the *Pot-au-Feu* simmer gently for about 2-3 hours. The beef should become tender and the flavors meld together.

5. If using potatoes, add them to the pot during the last 30 minutes of cooking, allowing them to cook until tender.

6. Once the beef is fork-tender and the vegetables are cooked, carefully remove them from the pot and arrange them on a serving platter. Discard the bouquet garni.

7. Slice the beef into thick pieces and place it alongside the vegetables on the serving platter.

8. Ladle some of the flavorful broth into bowls and serve it as a first course or soup.

9. Serve the Pot-au-Feu with Dijon mustard, crusty bread, and chopped parsley on the side.

Serve Pot-au-Feu in multiple courses, starting with the broth and vegetables and ending with the beef as the main course. It is a wonderful, comforting meal that is perfect for colder days.

Cassoulet

Cassoulet is a classic French dish originating from the region of Languedoc. It is a hearty and flavorful stew renowned for combining meats (duck confit, pork sausages, or lamb), beans, and a savory broth infused with garlic, tomatoes, and herbs like thyme and bay leaves. The slow cooking process melds the flavors, resulting in a robust and comforting dish embodying French provincial cuisine's warmth. Cassoluet's reputation as a heart-warming and indulgent comfort food has made it a cherished classic in its region and beyond.

Ingredients

- 1 pound dried white beans (Great Northern or Cannellini), soaked overnight
- 1 pound boneless pork shoulder, cut into chunks
- 4 duck legs confit or 4 duck thighs
- 4 sausages (such as Toulouse sausage or another garlic sausage)
- 8 ounces pancetta or bacon, diced
- 2 onions, finely chopped
- 4 cloves garlic, minced
- 2 carrots, diced
- 2 celery stalks, diced
- 1 can (14 ounces) diced tomatoes
- 2 tablespoons tomato paste
- 4 cups chicken or beef broth
- Bouquet garni (a bundle of herbs like thyme, parsley, and bay leaves, tied together)
- Salt and freshly ground black pepper
- 2 cups fresh breadcrumbs
- Chopped fresh parsley for garnish

Instructions

1. Preheat your oven to 300°F (150°C).

2. Drain and rinse the soaked beans. Place them in a large pot, cover with water, and bring to a boil. Reduce the heat and simmer for about 30-40 minutes until the beans are slightly

tender. Drain and set aside.

3. In a large Dutch oven or heavy-bottomed pot, cook the diced pancetta or bacon over medium heat until it releases fat and starts to brown. Remove the pancetta/bacon and set it aside.

4. In the same pot with the rendered fat, brown the chunks of pork shoulder in batches until golden on all sides. Remove and set aside.

5. Brown the sausages in the same pot, then remove and set aside.

6. In the same pot, sauté the onions, garlic, carrots, and celery until they begin to soften, about 5-6 minutes. Stir in the tomato paste and diced tomatoes. Cook for another 5 minutes, stirring occasionally.

7. Return the cooked beans, pork shoulder, pancetta/bacon, and sausages to the pot. Pour in the chicken or beef broth. Add the bouquet garni. Season with salt and pepper. Bring the mixture to a simmer, cover the pot, and transfer it to the preheated oven. Cook for about 2-3 hours, occasionally stirring gently, until the beans and meats are tender and flavors meld together.

8. In a separate pan, toast the breadcrumbs until golden brown.

9. Once the cassoulet is done cooking, remove it from the oven. Discard the bouquet garni.

10. Sprinkle the toasted breadcrumbs over the top of the cassoulet. Increase the oven temperature to 375°F (190°C). Return the cassoulet to the oven and bake for an additional 15-20 minutes until the breadcrumbs form a golden crust.

11. Serve the cassoulet hot, garnished with chopped fresh parsley, and serve with crusty bread.

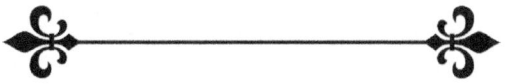

Blanquette de Veau

This timeless dish, featuring succulent veal simmered in a velvety white wine and stock sauce, captures the essence of comfort and sophistication. Crowned with a rich creaminess and a hint of citrus, each tender morsel of veal invites you to experience the epitome of culinary finesse. Elevate your dining experience with this classic French masterpiece, a true celebration of gastronomic delight.

Ingredients

- 2 pounds (about 1 kg) veal shoulder or stew meat, cut into cubes
- 1 onion, finely chopped
- 2 carrots, peeled and sliced
- 2 leeks, white and light green parts only, sliced
- 2 cloves garlic, minced
- 1 bouquet garni (a bundle of fresh herbs such as thyme, parsley, and bay leaves, tied together)
- 1 cup dry white wine
- 4 cups veal or chicken stock
- Salt and black pepper to taste
- 1/2 cup all-purpose flour
- 1/2 cup unsalted butter
- 1 cup pearl onions, peeled
- 1 cup button mushrooms, cleaned and halved
- 1 cup heavy cream
- 2 tablespoons lemon juice
- Fresh parsley, chopped, for garnish

Instructions

1. In a large pot, melt half of the butter over medium-high heat. Add the veal cubes and brown them on all sides. Remove the veal and set it aside.

2. In the same pot, add the remaining butter. Sauté the chopped onion, sliced carrots, leeks, and minced garlic until softened.

3. Sprinkle the flour over the vegetables and stir well to create a roux.

4. Gradually pour in the white wine and stock, stirring constantly to avoid lumps. Add the bouquet garni, salt, and black pepper.

5. Return the browned veal to the pot. Bring the mixture to a gentle simmer, then cover and let it cook over low heat for about 1.5 to 2 hours or until the veal is tender.

6. In a separate pan, blanch the pearl onions in boiling water for a few minutes, then peel off the skins.

7. In another pan, sauté the mushrooms in a bit of butter until they are golden brown.

8. Add the pearl onions and mushrooms to the veal stew. Simmer for an additional 15-20 minutes.

9. Stir in the heavy cream and lemon juice. Adjust the seasoning if needed.

10. Remove the bouquet garni and discard it.

11. Serve the Blanquette de Veau hot, garnished with fresh chopped parsley. It pairs wonderfully with rice, potatoes, or crusty bread.

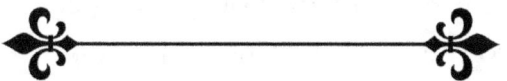

Chapter Seven

Gourmet Courtiers
Sides and Accompaniments

In the lavish salons and bustling kitchens of Napoleonic France, a culinary revolution unfolded, as rich in flavor as it was in historical significance. One overlooked aspect of this vibrant cultural evolution is the world of sides and accompaniments. Often overshadowed by grand entrees, these unsung heroes complemented the grandeur of the main courses and defined the art of dining during that illustrious period. The era was a crucible where the flames of culinary innovation and tradition danced together.

Side dishes and accompaniments in Napoleonic cuisine were not merely supporting actors but integral components that added depth, contrast, and richness to dining experiences. Each category unveiled a world of culinary craftsmanship, from the vibrant colors of fresh vegetables to the intricate sauces. The essence of Napoleonic fare lies in the harmonious orchestration of ingredients and methods—a symphony conducted in kitchens across France. Through the careful selection of fresh produce, the finesse in techniques, and the regional variations that added depth to flavors, side dishes emerged as vibrant companions to main courses, embodying the essence of an era characterized by gastronomic excellence.

Gratin Dauphinois

Gratin Dauphinois makes a delightful side dish for roasts or hearty mains. Its creamy, comforting texture and rich flavor from the infused cream and garlic make it a beloved classic of French cuisine.

Ingredients

- 2 pounds (about 1 kg) Russet potatoes, peeled and thinly sliced (about 1/8 inch thick)
- 2 cups (475 ml) heavy cream
- 2 cloves garlic, minced or finely chopped
- 1 cup (100 g) grated Gruyère or Emmental cheese (optional)
- Salt and pepper to taste
- Butter for greasing the baking dish
- Nutmeg (optional, for additional flavor)

Instructions

1. Preheat your oven to 350°F (175°C). Grease a baking dish generously with butter.

2. In a saucepan, combine the heavy cream and minced garlic. Heat the mixture over medium heat until it's warm but not boiling. Let it infuse for a few minutes to allow the garlic flavor to infuse into the cream. You can add a pinch of nutmeg to the cream for extra flavor if desired.

3. Layer half of the sliced potatoes in the prepared baking dish, overlapping them slightly. Season the layer with salt and pepper.

4. Pour half of the warm garlic-infused cream over the first layer of potatoes, ensuring the cream covers them evenly.

5. Repeat with the second layer of potatoes, arranging them neatly and seasoning again with salt and pepper.

6. Pour the remaining cream mixture over the second layer of potatoes, ensuring all the potatoes are covered.

7. If using, sprinkle the grated cheese evenly over the top of the dish.

8. Cover the baking dish with foil and place it in the preheated oven. Bake for about 45-55 minutes. After 30 minutes, remove the foil to allow the top to brown and the potatoes to cook through.

9. Check for doneness by inserting a knife into the potatoes; they should be tender.

10. Once cooked, remove the gratin from the oven and let it rest for a few minutes before serving.

Haricots Verts

This dish highlights the natural flavor of green beans with the aromatic blend of garlic and shallots. It is a simple yet elegant way to enjoy the freshness and vibrancy of haricots verst, making it a perfect addition to any meal.

Ingredients

- 1 pound (about 450g) haricots verts (French green beans), trimmed
- 2 tablespoons unsalted butter
- 2 cloves garlic, minced
- 1 shallot, finely chopped
- 1/4 cup (60ml) vegetable or chicken broth
- Salt and pepper to taste
- Fresh parsley for garnish (optional)

Instructions

1. Prepare the haricots verts by rinsing them under cold water and trimming off the ends if needed. Pat them dry with a clean kitchen towel.

2. In a large skillet or sauté pan, melt the butter over medium heat.

3. Add the minced garlic and chopped shallot to the melted butter. Sauté for 1-2 minutes until fragrant and the shallots become translucent, being careful not to let the garlic brown.

4. Add the trimmed haricots verts to the skillet. Toss them in the butter, garlic, and shallots for a minute or so to coat them evenly.

5. Pour the vegetable or chicken broth into the skillet. Cover with a lid and let the green beans cook for about 8-10 minutes, stirring occasionally.

6. Check for doneness by tasting a bean; they should be tender but still have a slight crispness.

7. Season the haricots verts with salt and pepper to taste. If you prefer, garnish with fresh parsley before serving for added freshness.

8. Serve the Haricots Verts hot as a delightful side dish alongside your favorite main course.

Ratatouille Napoléonienne

Ratatouille Napoléonienne presents the classic flavors of ratatouille in a visually striking manner, with layers of colorful vegetables that celebrate the essence of Provence. Enjoy the medley of textures and flavors in this elegant dish that pays homage to both traditions and creativity.

Ingredients

- 1 large eggplant, thinly sliced
- 2 zucchinis, thinly sliced lengthwise
- 2 large tomatoes, thinly sliced
- 1 red bell pepper, thinly sliced
- 1 yellow bell pepper, thinly sliced
- 1 onion, thinly sliced
- 4 cloves garlic, minced
- 3 tablespoons olive oil
- 1 tablespoon tomato paste
- 1 teaspoon dried thyme
- 1 teaspoon dried oregano
- Salt and pepper to taste
- Fresh basil leaves for garnish

Instructions

1. Preheat your oven to 375°F (190°C).

2. Heat 1 tablespoon of olive oil in a skillet over medium heat. Sauté the minced garlic and thinly sliced onion until softened and fragrant.

3. Add the tomato paste to the skillet and cook for a minute, stirring to incorporate.

4. Spread the garlic, onion, and tomato paste mixture evenly on the bottom of a baking dish to create the base layer.

5. Arrange the thinly sliced vegetables in an overlapping pattern on top of the base layer, alternating between eggplant, zucchini, tomatoes, and bell peppers. Continue this layering until you've used all the vegetables, creating multiple layers.

6. Drizzle the remaining olive oil over the assembled vegetables. Sprinkle with dried thyme, dried oregano, salt, and pepper.

7. Cover the baking dish with foil and bake in the preheated oven for about 45-50 minutes, or until the vegetables are tender.

8. Once cooked, remove the foil and continue baking for an additional 10-15 minutes to lightly brown the top.

9. Let the Ratatouille Napoléonienne cool slightly before serving. Garnish with fresh basil leaves for a vibrant finish.

Asperges à la Crème

Asperges à la Crème offers a delightful way to enjoy asparagus's natural flavors complemented by the richness of a creamy sauce. It is a versatile dish that pairs wonderfully with various main courses or serves as an elegant appetizer.

Ingredients

- 1 pound (about 450g) fresh asparagus spears, trimmed
- 2 tablespoons unsalted butter
- 1 shallot, finely chopped
- 1/2 cup (120ml) heavy cream
- Salt and pepper to taste
- Fresh parsley or chives for garnish (optional)

Instructions

1. Bring a pot of salted water to a boil. Add the trimmed asparagus spears and cook for about 3-5 minutes, depending on their thickness, until they are tender yet still slightly crisp. Drain the asparagus and immediately plunge them into a bowl of ice water to stop the cooking process. This helps retain their vibrant color.

2. In a skillet or sauté pan, melt the butter over medium heat.

3. Add the finely chopped shallot to the melted butter and sauté until it becomes translucent and soft, but not browned.

4. Reduce the heat to low and pour in the heavy cream. Stir gently to combine with the shallots and butter.

5. Let the cream simmer and reduce slightly for a few minutes, allowing it to thicken slightly.

6. Season the cream sauce with salt and pepper to taste.

7. Arrange the blanched asparagus on a serving platter or individual plates.

8. Pour the creamy sauce over the asparagus spears, ensuring they are evenly coated.

9. Garnish with chopped fresh parsley or chives for a pop of color and added flavor.

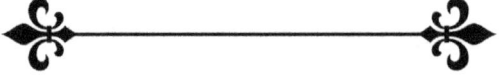

Épinards à la Crème

Épinards à la Crème offers a luxurious way to enjoy spinach's vibrant flavors complemented by the richness of the cream sauce. This versatile dish pairs wonderfully with various mains and is a delightful accompaniment to any meal.

Ingredients

- 1 pound (about 450g) fresh spinach leaves, washed and stemmed
- 2 tablespoons unsalted butter
- 2 cloves garlic, minced
- 1/2 cup (120ml) heavy cream
- Pinch of nutmeg (optional)
- Salt and pepper to taste

Instructions

1. In a large pot or skillet, melt the butter over medium heat.

2. Add the minced garlic to the melted butter and sauté for about a minute until fragrant, being careful not to let it brown.

3. Add the cleaned spinach leaves to the pot. You may need to add them in batches, allowing them to wilt down before adding more. Cook the spinach for about 2-3 minutes until it's wilted and tender.

4. Once the spinach is cooked, reduce the heat to low.

5. Pour the heavy cream over the cooked spinach, stirring gently to combine.

6. Let the cream simmer with the spinach for a few minutes, allowing the flavors to meld together. If using, add a pinch of nutmeg for additional flavor.

7. Season the dish with salt and pepper to taste.

8. Once the cream has slightly thickened and coated the spinach, remove the pot from the heat.

9. Serve the Épinards à la Crème hot as a delicious and creamy side dish.

Purée de Pommes de Terre

This Purée de Pommes de Terre (mashed potatoes) recipe yields creamy, buttery mashed potatoes that pair wonderfully with various dishes. Serve them alongside your favorite main dishes, or enjoy them alone as a comforting standalone side dish.

Ingredients

- 2 pounds (about 1 kg) Yukon Gold or Russet potatoes, peeled and cut into chunks
- 4 tablespoons unsalted butter, cut into cubes
- 1/2 cup (120ml) whole milk or heavy cream, warmed
- Salt and pepper to taste
- Chopped fresh chives or parsley for garnish (optional)

Instructions

1. Place the peeled and cut potatoes in a large pot and cover them with cold water. Add a generous pinch of salt to the water.

2. Bring the water to a boil, then reduce the heat to medium and let the potatoes simmer for about 15-20 minutes or until they are fork-tender.

3. Drain the cooked potatoes thoroughly and return them to the pot. This step helps remove excess moisture.

4. Using a potato masher or a potato ricer, mash the potatoes while they are still hot to ensure a smooth consistency.

5. Add the cubed butter to the hot mashed potatoes and stir until the butter melts and incorporates evenly.

6. Slowly pour in the warm milk or cream while continuing to mash or stir the potatoes. Keep adding the milk or cream until you achieve your desired creamy consistency. You can adjust the amount to your preference.

7. Season the purée generously with salt and pepper, tasting as you go to get the perfect balance of flavors.

8. Once well combined and seasoned, transfer the purée de pommes de terre to a serving bowl. Garnish with chopped fresh chives or parsley for an extra touch of flavor and color, if desired.

Fun Fact:
Napoleon became an ardent proponent of potatoes after research was released attesting to their nutritional value. The groundbreaking study that elevated the starchy tuber to the favor of the emperor was Antoine Parmentier's *Examen Chimique Des Pommes De Terre* (1773).

Petits Pois à la Française

This dish offers a delightful combination of tender peas in a flavorful sauce, making it a versatile and elegant side dish that complements various main courses.

Ingredients

- 1 pound (about 450g) fresh or frozen peas
- 2 tablespoons unsalted butter
- 1 small onion, finely chopped
- 1-2 cloves garlic, minced
- 1/2 cup (120ml) chicken or vegetable broth
- 1 tablespoon all-purpose flour
- 1/4 cup (60ml) heavy cream or crème fraîche (optional)
- Salt and pepper to taste
- Fresh parsley, chopped, for garnish (optional)

Instructions

1. If using fresh peas, blanch them in boiling water for a few minutes until they are bright green and slightly tender. If using frozen peas, thaw them according to package instructions.

2. In a saucepan or skillet, melt the butter over medium heat.

3. Add the finely chopped onion to the melted butter and sauté until it becomes translucent and soft.

4. Add the minced garlic to the pan and cook for another minute until fragrant.

5. Sprinkle the flour over the onion and garlic, stirring continuously for a minute to cook off the raw taste of the flour.

6. Slowly pour in the chicken or vegetable broth while stirring constantly to create a smooth sauce. Let it simmer for a couple of minutes to thicken slightly.

7. Add the peas to the sauce, stirring to coat them evenly. If using fresh peas, let them cook in the sauce for about 5-7 minutes until tender. If using frozen peas, they only need a couple of minutes to heat through.

8. Optional: Stir in the heavy cream or crème fraîche to the peas for extra richness and creaminess.

9. Season the peas with salt and pepper to taste.

10. Once cooked and coated with the flavorful sauce, remove the pan from heat.

11. Garnish the Petits Pois à la Française with chopped fresh parsley for a touch of freshness before serving.

Sauce Robert

Sauce Robert boasts a tangy and savory flavor profile that perfectly complements meats, particularly pork. It is a versatile sauce that adds depth and richness to various dishes.

Ingredients

- 1 tablespoon unsalted butter
- 1 tablespoon olive oil
- 1 small onion, finely chopped
- 1 cup (240ml) beef or veal stock
- 2 tablespoons Dijon mustard
- 2 tablespoons white wine vinegar
- 1 teaspoon sugar
- Salt and pepper to taste
- Chopped fresh parsley for garnish (optional)

Instructions

1. In a saucepan, heat the butter and olive oil over medium heat.

2. Add the finely chopped onion to the pan and sauté until it becomes soft and translucent, but not browned.

3. Pour in the beef or veal stock, and let it simmer with the onions for a few minutes to reduce slightly.

4. Stir in the Dijon mustard, white wine vinegar, and sugar, combining everything well. Allow the sauce to simmer gently for about 10-15 minutes, stirring occasionally, until it thickens to your desired consistency.

5. Taste the sauce and season with salt and pepper according to your preference. Once the sauce has reached the desired thickness and the flavors have melded, remove it from heat. Optionally, garnish the Sauce Robert with chopped fresh parsley before serving.

Chapter Eight

Sweet Conquests
Desserts

In the heart of 18th-century France, amidst the political upheavals and grandeur of the Napoleonic era, a tantalizing revolution was quietly underway. The sumptuous layers of influence, innovation, and decadence characterized the desserts enjoyed by the elite and commoners during Napoleon's reign. It is an exploration of the nexus where French culinary tradition met creativity and advancement, where the mastery of pastry chefs competed with the quest for new and exotic flavors. From the elegant salons of Paris to the sprawling estates of the countryside, desserts were not merely confections but cultural symbols, status markers, and, most importantly, sensory delights.

Before Napoleon's ascension, desserts had already begun a journey of refinement and sophistication. The royal courts of Versailles had long been the epicenter of culinary extravagance, where lavish feasts and delicate pastries were integral to courtly life. However, under Napoleon's rule, confections underwent a renaissance, transcending the confines of the elite circles to permeate wider society. Delicate pastries, such as éclairs, mille-feuille, and macarons, were already making their mark in the pre-Napoleonic era, showcasing the ingenuity of French pastry chefs. Yet, Napoleon's shifting political and social landscape propelled these delicacies into the limelight.

The democratization of desserts under Napoleon's rule was noteworthy. While previously reserved for the aristocracy and the affluent, these indulgences became more accessible to a broader section of society. Bakeries and patisseries began cropping up in urban centers, offering an array of delectable treats that were not solely the privilege of the elite. The evolution of dessert culture mirrored societal shifts. It reflected the changing roles of women in the kitchen, the advancements in culinary technology, and the exploration of new and exotic ingredients brought about by global exploration and trade. Despite these significant strides, desserts often served as indicators of social standing in the socially stratified society of Napoleon's era. The opulence and variety of desserts presented at gatherings and feasts were not just culinary delights but reflections of one's wealth and sophistication. Elaborate *pièces montées (*grand centerpiece confections) showcased a host's affluence and culinary appreciation. In contrast, the working class indulged in simple sweets like bread pudding or fruit-based desserts, highlighting the socioeconomic divide that permeated after-dinner treats.

Desserts played a pivotal role in shaping social interactions and fostering connections within society. Afternoon tea gatherings, known as goûter in France, offered a space for socialization, where desserts like madeleines, éclairs, and petits fours accompanied conversations and shared moments. Similarly, dessert courses at formal dinners and soirées were not just about culinary indulgence but also about social etiquette. Strict rules governed the serving and presentation of confections, reflecting the refinement and decorum expected in high society.

The era of Napoleon witnessed a confluence of innovation and tradition in dessert-making techniques. Pastry chefs embraced new methods while honoring classical principles, resulting in a renaissance of flavors and textures. Pursuing dessert perfection led to fierce rivalries and collaborative endeavors among pastry chefs. Competition fueled innovation as chefs vied to create the most exquisite and innovative delicacies to impress their patrons. Collaborations also yielded remarkable results as exchanging ideas, techniques, and ingredients led to new sweet creations. This spirit of cooperation propelled the evolution of desserts and fostered a sense of camaraderie among culinary artisans.

Exploration and global trade routes during Napoleon's era played a pivotal role in expanding the repertoire of confectionary components. While staples like butter, sugar, and flour formed the foundation of many indulgences, the influx of ingredients from distant lands brought novel tastes and textures to the table. Introducing tropical fruits like pineapples and mangoes added a vibrant, exotic touch to desserts, elevating their sensory appeal. Meanwhile, using almonds, hazelnuts, and pistachios in various forms, from marzipan to nougat, highlighted nuts' versatility. The spice trade brought an array of aromatic zests like cinnamon, cardamom, and cloves to the shores of France, infusing delights with fragrant and nuanced seasonings. The emergence of chocolate as a sought-after commodity revolutionized dessert-making. From the rich, velvety consistency of ganache to the decadence of chocolate cakes and pastries, this discovery from the Americas captured the imagination of pastry chefs and became a hallmark of

French delectables.

The arrival of indulgent confections marked the sweet crescendo of a meal during the French Empire. The desserts of Napoleon's time continue to cast a long shadow over the world of culinary arts, their influence extending far beyond the borders of time. The techniques, recipes, and flavors introduced during this era continue to inspire contemporary pastry chefs worldwide. Their legacy lives on in the sweet creations that grace our tables today, a testament to the artistry, innovation, and cultural significance of a period that revolutionized the very essence of desserts.

Mille-Feuille (Thousand Leaves)

Napoleon Bonaparte had a penchant for several desserts that became synonymous with his imperial court. Among the sweet treasures of Frech patisserie, one iconic dessert stands out as a testament to culinary artistry and historical significance—the Napoleon cake, also known as Mille-Feuille. Layers of delicate puff pastry sandwiching rich pastry cream, topped with a glossy layer of caramelized sugar, made this dessert a staple at the emperor's table.

Ingredients

For the Pastry

- 1 sheet puff pastry (store-bought or homemade)
- Powdered sugar for dusting

For the Pastry Cream

- 2 cups whole milk
- 1 teaspoon vanilla extract or 1 vanilla bean (seeds scraped)
- 4 egg yolks
- 1/2 cup granulated sugar
- 1/4 cup cornstarch
- Pinch of salt
- 2 tablespoons unsalted butter

For the Glaze

- 1 cup powdered sugar
- 2-3 tablespoons water
- 1 teaspoon vanilla extract

Instructions

1. Prepare the Pastry

- Preheat your oven to 400°F (200°C).
- Roll out the puff pastry sheet to about 1/4 inch thickness on a floured surface.
- Cut the pastry into three equal-sized rectangles. Prick the rectangles with a fork to prevent excessive rising.
- Place the pastry rectangles on a baking sheet lined with parchment paper and bake for about 15-20 minutes until golden brown and puffed.
- Remove from the oven and allow them to cool completely.

2. Make the Pastry Cream

- In a saucepan, heat the milk and vanilla over medium heat until it just begins to simmer. Do not boil.
- In a separate bowl, whisk together the egg yolks, sugar, cornstarch, and a pinch of salt until well combined.
- Slowly pour the hot milk into the egg mixture while whisking continuously to temper the eggs.
- Pour the mixture back into the saucepan and cook over medium heat, whisking constantly until it thickens and comes to a boil.
- Remove from heat, stir in the butter until melted, and transfer the pastry cream to a bowl. Cover the surface with plastic wrap to prevent a skin from forming. Chill in the refrigerator for about an hour until completely cool.

3. Assemble the Mille-Feuille

- Once the pastry and pastry cream have cooled, place one pastry rectangle on a serving plate. Dust it lightly with powdered sugar.
- Spread a generous layer of pastry cream evenly over the first pastry layer.

- Place the second pastry rectangle on top and repeat the process with another layer of pastry cream.
- Top with the third pastry rectangle. Lightly dust the top with powdered sugar.

4. Prepare the Glaze and Serve

- In a small bowl, mix powdered sugar, water, and vanilla extract until you achieve a smooth, pourable consistency.
- Drizzle the glaze over the top pastry layer, allowing it to drip down the sides of the mille-feuille.
- Refrigerate the assembled mille-feuille for at least 1-2 hours before serving to allow the layers to set.

Ile Flottante (Floating Island)

The ethereal Ile Flottante (Floating Island) was a dessert of delicate poached meringue adrift in a sea of crème anglaise. Its lightness and subtle sweetness offered a delightful contrast to the richness of other imperial desserts, demonstrating the finesse of French pastry craftsmanship.

Ingredients

For the Meringue

- 4 egg whites
- 1/2 cup granulated sugar
- 1 teaspoon vanilla extract
- Pinch of salt

For the Crème Anglaise

- 4 egg yolks
- 1/4 cup granulated sugar
- 2 cups whole milk
- 1 teaspoon vanilla extract

For Serving

- Caramel sauce (optional)
- Toasted slivered almonds (optional)

Instructions

1. Prepare the Meringue

- In a clean, dry mixing bowl, whisk the egg whites with a pinch of salt until they form stiff peaks.
- Gradually add the sugar while continuing to whisk until the meringue is glossy and holds stiff peaks.
- Stir in the vanilla extract gently until combined.

2. Poach the Meringue

- In a wide saucepan or skillet, bring water to a gentle simmer.
- Using a spoon or a small ice cream scoop, shape the meringue into oval or round quenelles and carefully drop them into the simmering water.
- Poach the meringues for about 2-3 minutes on each side until they are firm but still light and airy. Remove them with a slotted spoon and place them on a paper towel to drain excess water. Set aside.

3. Prepare the Crème Anglaise

- In a separate bowl, whisk together the egg yolks and sugar until pale and creamy.
- In a saucepan, heat the milk over medium heat until it just begins to simmer. Remove from heat.
- Slowly pour a small amount of the hot milk into the egg yolk mixture, whisking constantly to temper the eggs.

- Gradually add the tempered egg mixture back into the saucepan with the remaining hot milk, whisking continuously.
- Return the saucepan to low heat and cook the mixture, stirring constantly with a wooden spoon, until it thickens and coats the back of the spoon. Do not let it boil.
- Remove from heat, strain the crème Anglaise through a fine-mesh sieve into a bowl, and stir in the vanilla extract. Let it cool.

4. Assemble and Serve

- Pour the cooled crème anglaise into serving dishes.
- Place the poached meringues on top of the crème anglaise and serve at room temperature.
- Optionally, drizzle caramel sauce over the meringues and sprinkle toasted slivered almonds on top for added flavor and texture.

Crème Brûlée

Delight in the epitome of French dessert elegance with this Crème Brûlée recipe. This iconic custard, characterized by its silky smooth texture and crisp caramelized top, is a symphony of indulgence for the senses. With each spoonful, savor the rich vanilla-infused cream that melts delicately on the tongue, juxtaposed by the satisfying crackle of caramelized sugar. As timeless as it is luxurious, Crème Brûlée epitomizes the art of French patisserie, inviting you to savor moments of pure decadence and culinary refinement.

Ingredients

- 6 large egg yolks
- 1/2 cup granulated sugar (plus extra for caramelizing)
- 2 cups heavy cream
- 1 teaspoon vanilla extract
- Pinch of salt

Instructions

1. Preheat and Prepare

- Preheat your oven to 300°F (150°C).
- Arrange six ramekins or custard dishes in a baking dish or roasting pan with high sides. Set aside.

2. Prepare the Custard Base

- In a mixing bowl, whisk together the egg yolks and sugar until the mixture is thick and pale yellow.

3. Heat the Cream Mixture

- In a saucepan, heat the heavy cream over medium heat until it just starts to simmer. Do not boil.
- Remove the cream from heat and gradually pour it into the egg yolk mixture, whisking continuously to temper the eggs.

4. Flavor the Custard

- Stir in the vanilla extract and a pinch of salt into the cream and egg mixture until well combined.

5. Fill and Bake

- Strain the custard mixture through a fine-mesh sieve to ensure a smooth texture.
- Divide the custard evenly among the ramekins placed in the baking dish.

- Pour hot water into the baking dish, around the ramekins, until it reaches about halfway up the sides of the ramekins. This water bath helps the custards bake evenly.

6. Bake the Crème Brûlée

- Carefully transfer the baking dish to the preheated oven.
- Bake for approximately 35-40 minutes until the edges are set but the center still jiggles slightly when gently shaken.

7. Chill the Custards

- Remove the baking dish from the oven and carefully lift the ramekins out of the water bath. Allow them to cool to room temperature.
- Once cooled, cover each ramekin with plastic wrap and refrigerate for at least 4 hours or overnight to set completely.

8. Caramelize the Sugar Topping

- Just before serving, sprinkle a thin, even layer of granulated sugar on top of each custard.
- Use a kitchen torch to caramelize the sugar by moving the flame in a circular motion until the sugar melts and turns golden brown. Alternatively, place the custards under a broiler for a few minutes until the sugar caramelizes.

9. Serve and Enjoy

- Allow the caramelized sugar to cool and harden for a minute before serving.
- Serve the classic Crème Brûlée immediately, allowing the contrast between the crisp caramelized topping and the creamy custard to delight your taste buds.

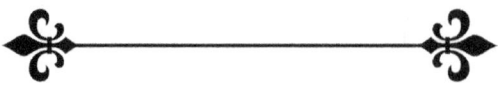

Baba au Rhum

This decadent dessert originated in the grand kitchens of Parisian palaces and combines the delicate texture of brioche with the indulgent allure of rum-infused syrup. Each golden pastry, soaked to perfection, creates a symphony of flavors that dance on the palate with every bite. With its rich history and timeless elegance, Baba au Rhum embodies the essence of French culinary artistry. It offers a luxurious treat to delight and captivate even the most discerning palates.

Ingredients

For the Dough

- 2 1/4 teaspoons (1 packet) active dry yeast
- 1/4 cup warm water (about 110°F / 45°C)
- 2 cups all-purpose flour
- 3 large eggs
- 3 tablespoons granulated sugar
- 1/2 teaspoon salt
- 1/2 cup unsalted butter, softened

For the Syrup

- 1 cup water
- 1 cup granulated sugar
- 1 cup dark rum (or rum of your choice)

Instructions

1. Activate the Yeast

- In a small bowl, dissolve the yeast in warm water and let it sit for about 5-10 minutes until it becomes frothy.

2. Prepare the Dough

- In a mixing bowl, combine the flour, eggs, sugar, and salt. Mix until well combined.
- Add the softened butter and yeast mixture to the bowl. Knead the dough by hand or with a stand mixer fitted with a dough hook until it becomes smooth and elastic about 10-15 minutes.
- Cover the dough with a clean cloth and let it rise in a warm, draft-free place for about 1-2 hours until it doubles in size.

3. Shape the Babas

- Grease a baba mold or small individual cake molds.
- Punch down the risen dough and divide it into equal portions. Shape each portion into small balls and place them into the prepared molds.
- Cover the molds again with a cloth and let the dough rise for an additional 30-45 minutes.

4. Bake the Babas

- Preheat your oven to 375°F (190°C).
- Bake the babas for approximately 15-20 minutes or until they turn golden brown and are cooked through.
- Remove the babas from the oven and let them cool slightly.

5. Prepare the Rum Syrup

- In a saucepan, combine water and sugar. Bring the mixture to a gentle boil, stirring until the sugar dissolves.
- Remove the saucepan from heat and stir in the dark rum. Let the syrup cool to room temperature.

6. Soak the Babas and Serve

- Place the slightly cooled babas in a shallow dish or a tray that has a bit of depth.
- Pour the cooled rum syrup over the warm babas, allowing them to soak up the syrup. You can use a spoon to ladle the syrup over the babas multiple times to ensure they absorb it thoroughly.
- Once the babas have soaked up the syrup, they are ready to be served. They can be served plain or with a dollop of whipped cream or fresh fruit on top.

Profiteroles au Chocolat

These delicate choux pastry puffs filled with velvety vanilla pastry cream and drizzled with a luscious chocolate ganache originated in the heart of French patisseries. Each bite offers a symphony of textures and flavors, as the crisp exterior gives way to the creamy richness within. Perfectly paired with a cup of coffee or as a sumptuous dessert, Profiteroles au Chocolat epitomizes the art of French pastry, inviting you to savor moments of indulgence and delight.

Ingredients

For the Choux Pastry

- 1/2 cup water
- 1/4 cup unsalted butter
- 1/2 cup all-purpose flour
- 2 large eggs, at room temperature

For the Cream Filling

- 1 cup heavy cream
- 2 tablespoons powdered sugar
- 1 teaspoon vanilla extract

For the Chocolate Sauce

- 1/2 cup dark chocolate (chopped or chips)
- 1/2 cup heavy cream
- 2 tablespoons powdered sugar
- 1 teaspoon vanilla extract

Instructions

1. Prepare the Choux Pastry

- Preheat your oven to 425°F (220°C). Line a baking sheet with parchment paper.
- In a saucepan, combine water and butter. Bring it to a boil over medium heat.
- Reduce the heat to low, add the flour all at once, and stir vigorously with a wooden spoon until the mixture forms a smooth ball of dough that pulls away from the sides of the pan.
- Remove the pan from the heat and let it cool for a couple of minutes.
- Add the eggs one at a time, beating well after each addition, until the dough becomes smooth and glossy.

2. Pipe and Bake the Profiteroles

- Transfer the choux pastry dough into a piping bag fitted with a round tip (or simply use a spoon).
- Pipe small mounds (about 1-1.5 inches in diameter) onto the prepared baking sheet, leaving space between each mound.
- Bake in the preheated oven for 15 minutes, then reduce the heat to 375°F (190°C) and bake for an additional 10-15 minutes until they are golden brown and puffed. Avoid opening the oven door while baking.

3. Prepare the Cream Filling

- In a mixing bowl, whip the heavy cream, powdered sugar, and vanilla extract until stiff peaks form.
- Transfer the whipped cream into a piping bag fitted with a small tip (or simply cut a small hole in a corner of a plastic bag).

4. Fill the Profiteroles

- Once the profiteroles have cooled, use a small knife to make a small slit or hole in the side of each profiterole.
- Pipe the whipped cream into the profiteroles through the hole until they are filled.

5. Make the Chocolate Sauce

- In a microwave-safe bowl or a saucepan, heat the heavy cream until it just starts to simmer.
- Pour the hot cream over the chopped chocolate. Let it sit for a minute, then stir until the chocolate is melted and the mixture is smooth. Stir in the powdered sugar and vanilla extract.

6. Assemble and Serve

- Drizzle the chocolate sauce generously over the filled profiteroles. Add whipped cream for extra decadence.
- Serve immediately, allowing the chocolate sauce to slightly set before indulging in these delightful profiteroles au chocolat.

Sabayon à la Champagne

Sabayon à la Champagne is a delightful and light dessert featuring a frothy, custard-like sauce made with Champagne. The delicate flavors of Champagne complement the richness of the egg yolks in a classic sabayon, creating a sophisticated dessert that is perfect for special occasions or a luxurious treat at the end of a meal.

Ingredients

- 6 large egg yolks
- 1/2 cup granulated sugar
- 1/2 cup Champagne or sparkling wine
- Fresh berries (such as strawberries, raspberries, or blueberries) for serving

Instructions

1. Prepare a Double Boiler

- Fill a saucepan with a couple of inches of water and bring it to a gentle simmer over medium-low heat.
- Place a heatproof bowl (preferably stainless steel or glass) over the saucepan, ensuring the bottom of the bowl doesn't touch the water.

2. Whisk Egg Yolks and Sugar

- In the heatproof bowl, whisk together the egg yolks and granulated sugar until well combined and slightly thickened.

3. Add Champagne

- Slowly pour the Champagne or sparkling wine into the egg yolk mixture while whisking continuously.

4. Cook the Sabayon

- Place the bowl over the simmering water (double boiler) and continue whisking gently but constantly. Be careful not to let the mixture overheat or the eggs will scramble.
- Continue whisking for about 8-10 minutes until the sabayon thickens and becomes frothy. It should coat the back of a spoon and hold a ribbon-like trail when lifted.

5. Serve

- Once the sabayon is cooked to your desired consistency, remove it from the heat.
- Divide the sabayon into serving dishes or glasses.
- Serve the sabayon warm or chilled, garnished with fresh berries on top.

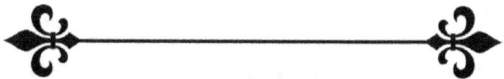

Nougat de Montélimar

Originating from the picturesque town of Montélimar, this iconic confection embodies the essence of Mediterranean indulgence. Crafted from golden honey, toasted almonds, and fluffy egg whites, each delicate bite of Nougat de Montélimar offers a symphony of textures and flavors, evoking the warmth of Provencal summers. With its centuries-old tradition and artisanal craftsmanship, this cherished sweet delicacy captures the heart and soul of French gastronomy. Whether shared among loved ones or savored as a personal indulgence, Nougat de Montélimar promises pure bliss and culinary delight.

Ingredients

- 1 1/4 cups almonds, whole, skin-on
- 1 1/4 cups pistachios, shelled
- 1 1/4 cups hazelnuts, whole
- 1 1/4 cups honey
- 2 cups granulated sugar
- 1/4 cup water
- 2 large egg whites
- Edible rice paper (optional for lining the pan)

Instructions

1. Prepare the Nuts

- Preheat your oven to 350°F (175°C).
- Spread the almonds, pistachios, and hazelnuts on separate baking sheets.
- Toast them in the preheated oven for about 8-10 minutes until lightly golden and fragrant. Keep an eye on them as they can quickly burn. Once done, set them aside to cool.

2. Prepare the Honey Syrup

- In a large saucepan, combine the honey, sugar, and water.
- Stir the mixture over medium heat until the sugar dissolves completely. Use a candy thermometer to monitor the temperature. You're aiming for the soft-ball stage, which is around 260°F (127°C).

3. Whip Egg Whites

- While the syrup is heating, use a stand mixer or hand mixer to whip the egg whites until they form stiff peaks.

4. Combine the Mixtures

- Once the syrup reaches the desired temperature, carefully pour it into the whipped egg whites in a slow, steady stream while continuously beating at medium speed. Be cautious as the syrup will be extremely hot.

- Continue to beat the mixture until it becomes thick and glossy, resembling a meringue consistency.

5. Fold in Nuts

- Gently fold in the toasted almonds, pistachios, and hazelnuts into the honey and egg white mixture until evenly distributed.

6. Prepare the Pan

- Line a square or rectangular pan with edible rice paper, if using. This helps with easy removal of the nougat once it sets.

7. Shape and Set

- Transfer the nougat mixture to the prepared pan and spread it evenly using a spatula or lightly oiled hands.
- Allow the nougat to cool and set at room temperature for several hours or preferably overnight until firm.

8. Cut and Serve

- Once the nougat has set completely, use a sharp knife to cut it into squares or rectangles.
- Store the nougat pieces in an airtight container, placing parchment paper between layers to prevent sticking.

Calissons

Indulge in the exquisite taste of Provence with Calissons, a beloved French confection that embodies centuries of tradition and craftsmanship. Originating from the sun-kissed region of Southern France, Calissons are delicately sweet almond candies adorned with a luscious layer of royal icing. Their unique diamond shape and fragrant notes of orange blossom water transport the senses to the picturesque landscapes of Provence. Perfect for special occasions or gifts, Calissons are a true embodiment of French artisanal mastery and gastronomic delight.

Ingredients

For the Calisson Paste

- 1 1/2 cups blanched almonds (ground)
- 1 cup powdered sugar
- 1/4 cup candied melon, finely chopped
- 1/4 cup candied orange peel, finely chopped
- 1/2 teaspoon almond extract
- 1 tablespoon orange blossom water
- 1 egg white

For the Icing

- 1 cup powdered sugar
- 1 tablespoon lemon juice
- Water (if needed for consistency)

Instructions

1. Prepare the Calisson Paste

- In a food processor, grind the blanched almonds until finely powdered.
- Add the powdered sugar, candied melon, candied orange peel, almond extract, and orange blossom water to the ground almonds. Pulse until well combined.

- Add the egg white and process again until a smooth, pliable paste forms.

2. Shape the Calissons

- Dust a work surface with powdered sugar. Roll out the calisson paste to about 1/4 inch thickness.
- Use a calisson cutter or a sharp knife to cut the paste into oval shapes. Alternatively, you can create oval shapes by hand.
- Place the shaped calissons on a parchment-lined baking sheet and let them dry for about 4-6 hours or overnight. This helps the calissons develop a slight crust.

3. Prepare the Icing and Apply

- In a bowl, combine the powdered sugar and lemon juice to create a thick icing. Add water, a teaspoon at a time, if needed, until you achieve a smooth and spreadable consistency.
- Once the calissons have dried, spread a thin layer of icing over the top of each calisson using a small spatula or the back of a spoon. Allow the icing to set.

4. Serve and Store

- Once the icing has set, the calissons are ready to be served.
- Store the calissons in an airtight container between layers of parchment paper to prevent sticking. They can be kept at room temperature for up to a week.

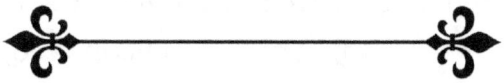

Chapter Nine

Vintage Ambitions
Libations

I n the tumultuous landscape of the Napoleonic era, there existed a seemingly mundane yet profoundly significant aspect of daily life: libations. In the clinking of glasses and the swirling of spirits, there lay a tapestry of culture, tradition, and social nuances that colored the lives of individuals across classes, continents, and battlefields. From the dusty vineyards of France to the bustling ports of Europe, from the revered halls of power to the humble haunts of the common folk, libations were more than just beverages—they were vessels of tradition, symbols of camaraderie, and echoes of a bygone era.

At the center of the era stood Napoleon, whose relationship with alcohol was as complex as his conquests. Known for his moderate drinking habits, the emperor was partial to fine wines, especially preferring champagne and Burgundy. His penchant for cognac and liqueurs, such as Chartreuse, showcased a taste for refinement amidst the tumultuous backdrop of his campaigns. Napoleon recognized alcohol's social and diplomatic significance. His moderation in drinking often contrasted with the excesses of his marshals and courtiers, portraying a deliberate image of control and discipline.

Wine: Nectar of Tradition

Wine, the elixir of Bacchus, held a revered position in the Napoleonic era. From Bordeaux's sun-soaked vineyards to Burgundy's terraced slopes, France reigned supreme as the heartland of wine production. The grand châteaus created vintages that adorned the tables of aristocrats and commoners alike, albeit in varying capacities. Wine was not just a beverage but a symbol of sophistication, status, and even patriotism. Varieties abounded—rich Bordeaux reds, delicate Burgundian Pinot Noirs, and the effervescent Champagnes—all found their place in the courts of Europe and the cups of soldiers in the field. The complexities of wine mirrored those of society, with nuances in taste reflecting regional differences and the social hierarchy.

Spirits: Essence of Conviviality

Beyond the realm of wine, spirits reigned supreme, each carrying its own character and story. Brandy, the favored spirit of France, found itself adorning the tables of both high society and the military. Gin, the quintessential British spirit, found its way into glasses far beyond the shores of England. Its aromatic juniper notes mingled with the tales of naval victories and the whispers of diplomatic negotiations. Rum, on the other hand, whispered tales of distant islands and maritime exploits, its history intertwined with the Caribbean and the bustling ports of trade.

Beer and Ale: Brews of the Common Folk

While wines and spirits took center stage in the higher echelons of society, beer and ale were the humble companions of the masses. These beverages were the lifeblood of European communities. From hearty stouts in England to crisp lagers in Germany, beer was more than a drink—it was a part of everyday life, sustaining laborers and thinkers alike. Alehouses served as the gathering spots to exchange news and forge friendships while laughter rang out amidst clinking glasses.

Aperitifs

During the Napoleonic era, aperitifs held a distinguished place in social gatherings and dining rituals. These pre-meal libations were not just beverages; they were elixirs crafted with finesse, chosen for their ability to stimulate the appetite and tantalize the senses. Aperitifs ranged from aromatic wines fortified with botanicals like vermouth and quinquina to herbal liqueurs like *génépi*, each bearing its unique blend of bitter, herbal, or fruity flavors. *Vin de Noix*, steeped in tradition, offered a nutty complexity believed to aid digestion, while absinthe, with its mysterious allure, danced on the fringes of acceptance. Aperitifs collectively formed a ritualistic prelude to meals, awakening palates and setting the stage for conviviality amidst the intricate tapestry of Napoleonic social customs.

In understanding the social and cultural importance of drinking during the era, we uncover not only the preferences for wines, spirits, and ales but also the importance of etiquette, the influence of war and politics, and the peculiar drinking habits of key historical figures. It is a story woven with threads of friendliness and camaraderie, reflecting the complexities of a time marked by upheaval and change amidst the clinking of glasses and the jovial banter governed by a nuanced code of behaviors and drinking traditions. These rituals were not merely formalities but intricate dances woven into social interactions, where each gesture and toast held more profound significance.

Toasting was an art form—a symphony of words and gestures that underscored the social fabric of the time. Whether in a grand salon or a modest tavern, toasts were a staple of gatherings. Each salute was a miniature performance, a moment of celebration or remembrance, binding individuals together in fellowship or allegiance. The choice of words was an exercise in diplomacy, expressing sentiments ranging from friendship to loyalty, admiration to respect. It was not uncommon for carefully crafted tributes to reflect the prevailing political sentiments or pay homage to influential figures.

The vessels from which libations flowed held symbolism. From ornate goblets to simple tankards, the choice conveyed the drinker's taste and social standing. The grandiosity of chalices and the simplicity of pewter mugs each told a story of the owner's place in society. Furthermore, their personalization, often adorned with family crests or emblems, added a layer of identity to the act of drinking. They were heirlooms, passed down through generations, carrying with them the memories and traditions of a lineage.

Beyond the formalities, various games, challenges, and customs accompanied alcoholic consumption. Drinking establishments were abuzz with activities ranging from dice games to rhyming challenges, each adding a layer of merriment to imbibing. Games were not solely for amusement; they also fostered connections and tested one's mettle. From card games to feats of endurance, these customs bound friends and comrades in shared experiences, creating bonds that transcended mere social gatherings.

Santé!

Noble Grapes: A Snapshot of French Wine History and Varietals

In the corridors of power, Napoleon's influence extended far beyond military conquests and legal reforms. His reign significantly impacted France's wine industry, shaping viticulture, viniculture, and the cultural perception of this revered beverage. Napoleon's rule ushered in a period of stability and organization, fostering an environment conducive to advancements. His administration implemented policies aimed at modernizing land ownership and standardizing the measurement systems, which, in turn, affected the structure and management of vineyards across France. Napoleon's emphasis on scientific progress led to the establishment of agricultural schools that taught innovative techniques in pruning, grafting, and vineyard management, paving the way for improved grape quality and yields.

One of the emperor's enduring legacies was the Napoleonic Code (1804), a comprehensive legal framework that revolutionized laws governing property, inheritance, and contracts. Within it lay provisions specifically addressing viticulture and trade, establishing regulations to ensure quality, protecting vineyard ownership, and standardizing wine production practices. The Code also delineated geographical boundaries and demarcated appellations, setting the stage for the eventual formalization of the *Appellation d'Origine Contrôlée* (AOC) system that would safeguard the authenticity and quality of French wines.

Amid political upheaval, winemaking traditions persevered, passed down through generations of vignerons and oenologists. The dedication to time-honored methods, such as manual harvesting and hand-sorting grapes, remained a hallmark of quality craftsmanship. Moreover, the era saw the emergence of notable figures whose contributions left an indelible mark on the world of wine. Visionaries like André Jullien, who authored pivotal works on winemaking, and renowned oenologists who pioneered scientific advancements in fermentation and wine chemistry elevated the understanding and practice of vinification. Cellar craftsmanship also reached new heights during this era, as cooperage became integral to winemaking. The science of barrel-making evolved, with coopers perfecting their craft to impart nuanced flavors and textures to wines. Carefully toasted and seasoned oak barrels became vessels of transformation, where wines matured and gained complexity.

Napoleon, a connoisseur of fine wines, appreciated wine's cultural significance. The finest vintages adorned his court, and he actively promoted French wines domestically and internationally. His patronage bolstered the prestige of specific wine regions, elevating their status among the aristocracy and foreign dignitaries. Through diplomatic channels and trade agreements, Napoleon facilitated the exportation of French wines to various corners of the globe, expanding their reach and solidifying France's position as a premier wine-producing nation.

Bordeaux: The Rise of the Grand Cru Classé

Bordeaux, a name synonymous with grandeur and excellence, boasted a viticultural history steeped in prestige. The Garonne and Dordogne rivers cradled vineyards that birthed some of the world's most celebrated wines. The Left Bank, with its illustrious communes of Médoc and Graves, birthed robust Cabernet Sauvignon-dominant blends, while the Right Bank, home to Pomerol and Saint-Émilion, crafted elegant Merlot-based wines. Under Napoleon's reign, Bordeaux experienced a resurgence as the classification concept emerged, laying the groundwork for the prestigious *Grand Cru Classé* (Great Classified Growth). The classification system codified quality and propelled Bordeaux onto the global stage as a benchmark of superiority.

Burgundy: Terroir, Tradition, and Transformations

In Burgundy, where the patchwork of vineyards reads like a mosaic, the concept of terroir (natural environment) reigned supreme. Napoleon's era witnessed a steadfast dedication to tradition, with the Côte de Nuits producing the regal Pinot Noir and the Côte de Beaune nurturing the delicate Chardonnay. Here, the walled vineyards held jealously guarded secrets, laying the groundwork for the intricate wine hierarchy observed today. Despite the political upheavals of the time, Burgundy held steadfast to its terroir-driven winemaking, a legacy that endures in every bottle.

Champagne: Bubbling Elegance in Uncertain Times

Champagne, the epitome of celebration and refinement, navigated turbulent waters during Napoleon's reign. Despite conflicts disrupting trade routes and threatening stability, the effervescent brew continued to sparkle in the glasses of nobles and socialites. The pioneering methods of Dom Pérignon and the emergence of Champagne houses laid the foundation for the *méthode champenoise* (champagne method), transforming still wines into the iconic bubbly elixir.

Napoleon's appreciation for this nectar only bolstered its reputation, solidifying Champagne as the drink of choice for moments of triumph and jubilation.

Rhône Valley: The Resilience of Southern Varietals

In the sun-kissed vineyards of the Rhône Valley, where the Mistral wind whispered through the vines, Grenache, Syrah, and Mourvèdre thrived. This southern bastion of viticulture weathered the storms of political change, showcasing the robust and flavorful wines of Châteauneuf-du-Pape and the elegant offerings of Côte-Rôtie. Tradition and innovation danced hand in hand as winemakers refined their craft, nurturing vines that bore testament to the rugged beauty of the terroir. The Rhône Valley, resilient and steadfast, preserved its identity amid the winds of change that swept through France during Napoleon's time.

Further Reading:

Philips, Roderick. *French Wine: A History*. Berkeley, CA: University of California Press, 2020.

Napoleon's Champagne Cup

Inspired by the grandeur of French imperial celebrations, this refreshing libation combines the effervescence of Champagne with a medley of vibrant fruits and aromatic spirits. Each sip offers a compelling blend of flavors and textures as the crisp bubbles mingle with the sweetness of fresh fruit and the subtle notes of liqueur. With its opulent presentation and rich historical significance, Napoleon's Champagne Cup is a tribute to the timeless allure of French gastronomy, inviting you to toast to moments of indulgence and sophistication.

Ingredients

- 1 sugar cube
- Angostura bitters
- 1 lemon twist
- 1 small piece of orange peel
- 1 oz brandy
- 4 oz chilled Champagne
- Crushed ice

Instructions

1. Begin by soaking the sugar cube with a few dashes of Angostura bitters.

2. Place the sugar cube at the bottom of a chilled Champagne flute.

3. Add a lemon twist and a small piece of orange peel to the flute.

4. Pour the brandy over the sugar cube and citrus peels.

5. Fill the glass with crushed ice.

6. Carefully top up the glass with chilled Champagne.

7. Gently stir the mixture to combine the flavors. Optionally, garnish with a lemon or orange twist.

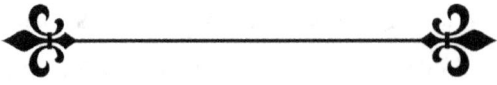

Napoleonic Era Punch

Inspired by the opulent gatherings and lavish celebrations of the period, this punch captures the essence of refinement and indulgence. Combining the finest spirits, fragrant spices, and luscious fruits, each sip offers a taste of sophistication and elegance reminiscent of the grand balls and soirées of Napoleon's court. Whether enjoyed as a centerpiece of social gatherings or as a nod to history's most illustrious moments, Napoleonic Era Punch invites you to raise a glass to the timeless pleasures of French tradition and camaraderie.

Ingredients

- 1 bottle (750ml) of brandy or rum
- 1 cup sugar (adjust to taste)
- 4 cups water
- 1 cup strong black tea (cooled)
- Juice of 4-5 lemons
- Juice of 2-3 oranges
- 1 nutmeg, grated
- Slices of lemon and orange for garnish
- Ice cubes (optional)
- A few dashes of bitters (optional)

Instructions

1. Start by boiling the water and dissolving the sugar in it to create a simple syrup. Allow it to cool.

2. Brew a strong cup of black tea and let it cool down as well.

3. In a large punch bowl, combine the brandy or rum, the cooled simple syrup, cooled black tea, and the freshly squeezed lemon and orange juices.

4. Grate a whole nutmeg into the mixture for added flavor. If you prefer, you can use pre-ground nutmeg, but fresh is always better.

5. If desired, add a few dashes of bitters for depth of flavor.

6. Stir the mixture well to ensure all the flavors are combined.

7. Add ice cubes to chill if serving immediately or refrigerate until ready to serve. Garnish the punch bowl with slices of lemon and orange.

Napoleonic Era Grog

Transport yourself to the windswept decks of Napoleonic-era ships with this authentic Napoleonic Era Grog recipe. Inspired by the seafaring traditions of the early 19th century, this invigorating concoction blends the robust flavors of rum, the tang of citrus, and the warmth of spices. Originally crafted to lift the spirits of sailors and ward off the chill of the sea, Napoleonic Era Grog remains a timeless classic, evoking tales of adventure and camaraderie. With each sip, relish in the echoes of maritime history and the enduring spirit of exploration that defines this beloved libation.

Ingredients

- 1 part dark rum (traditionally Navy rum)
- 3 parts hot water
- 1 tablespoon brown sugar (adjust to taste)
- Juice of half a lemon or lime
- Optional: Dash of nutmeg or cinnamon for garnish

Instructions

1. Heat the water until it's hot but not boiling.

2. In a sturdy mug or glass, pour in the dark rum.

3. Add the brown sugar and stir until it's dissolved.

4. Squeeze the juice of half a lemon or lime into the mug.

5. Pour the hot water into the mug over the rum, sugar, and citrus juice.

6. Stir the mixture gently to combine all the ingredients. Optionally, garnish with a dash of nutmeg or cinnamon for added flavor.

Napoleonic Era Mulled Wine

Step into the romantic ambiance of Napoleonic Europe with this evocative Napoleonic Era Mulled Wine recipe. Drawing inspiration from the cozy gatherings and festive revelries of the era, this aromatic concoction infuses robust red wine with an array of spices and citrus fruits, creating a soul-warming elixir fit for emperors and commoners alike. As the fragrant steam rises from each cup, let the tantalizing blend of cinnamon, cloves, and orange peel transport you to a bygone era of elegance and camaraderie.

Ingredients

- 1 bottle (750ml) of red wine (claret or Burgundy)
- 1/4 cup sugar (adjust to taste)
- 1 cinnamon stick
- 4-6 cloves
- Zest of 1 orange (in strips)
- Zest of 1 lemon (in strips)
- Juice of 1 orange
- Juice of 1 lemon
- Optional: 1/4 cup brandy or rum for added warmth

Instructions

1. Pour the red wine into a large saucepan or pot over low heat. Avoid boiling the wine, as it can affect the flavor.

2. Add the sugar, cinnamon stick, cloves, orange zest, and lemon zest to the wine.

3. Squeeze the juice of one orange and one lemon into the mixture.

4. Allow the wine and spices to gently simmer for about 20-30 minutes, ensuring it remains warm without boiling.

5. Taste the mulled wine and adjust the sweetness by adding more sugar if desired.

6. If using, stir in the brandy or rum just before serving for an extra kick.

7. Strain the mulled wine to remove the spices and citrus peels.

8. Serve the mulled wine warm in heat-resistant glasses or mugs.

Napoleonic Era Syllabub

This delightful dessert beverage, cherished for its airy texture and luxurious flavors, captures the essence of aristocratic indulgence. Combining rich cream, aromatic spices, and a splash of fortified wine, each spoonful of syllabub offers a taste of refined decadence and historical charm.

Ingredients

- 1 cup white wine or sherry
- 1/4 cup brandy or rum
- Zest and juice of 1 lemon
- Zest and juice of 1 orange
- 1/4 cup sugar (adjust to taste)
- 1 cup heavy cream
- Ground nutmeg or cinnamon for garnish

Instructions

1. In a bowl, combine the white wine or sherry with the brandy or rum.

2. Add the zest and juice of one lemon and one orange to the wine and spirits mixture.

3. Stir in the sugar until it dissolves completely.

4. In a separate bowl, whip the heavy cream until it reaches soft peaks.

5. Gently fold the wine and citrus mixture into the whipped cream. Do this slowly to maintain the fluffy texture of the cream.

6. Divide the syllabub mixture into individual serving glasses or bowls. Optionally, sprinkle a pinch of ground nutmeg or cinnamon on top for garnish.

Napoleonic Era Flip

This hearty libation, steeped in history and tradition, combines rich ale, warming spirits, and a touch of sweetness, creating a drink that embodies the spirit of conviviality and camaraderie. With its origins rooted in the bustling taverns of 18th-century Europe, the Napoleonic Era Flip invites you to savor the warmth of the hearth and the lively banter of companionship.

Ingredients

- 2 ounces dark ale or beer
- 2 ounces dark rum or brandy
- 1 tablespoon sugar or honey
- 1 whole egg
- Ground nutmeg or cinnamon for garnish

Instructions

1. Heat the beer or ale in a saucepan over low heat. Be careful not to let it boil.

2. In a separate bowl, beat the egg with the sugar or honey until it becomes frothy.

3. Slowly pour the heated beer into the bowl with the beaten egg and sugar mixture while continuously whisking to prevent curdling.

4. Pour the mixture back into the saucepan and add the rum or brandy.

5. Continuously stir the mixture over low heat until it becomes frothy and slightly thickened. Do not let it boil. Once heated through and frothy, pour the flip into a heat-resistant mug or glass. Optionally, sprinkle ground nutmeg or cinnamon on top for garnish.

Napoleonic Era Ratafia

Immerse yourself in the refined tastes of the Napoleonic era with this distinguished Napoleonic Era Ratafia recipe. This exquisite liqueur, steeped in history and elegance, captures the essence of sophistication and indulgence synonymous with the era. Crafted from the finest fruits, aromatic spices, and fortified wine, each sip of Ratafia evokes the opulent salons and grand soirées of Napoleonic France.

Ingredients

- 1 pound cherries (or another fruit like almonds, raspberries, etc.)
- 1 bottle (750ml) brandy or white wine
- 1 cup sugar (adjust to taste)
- Zest of 1 lemon and 1 orange
- Spices (optional): Cloves, cinnamon sticks, or other preferred spices

Instructions

1. Wash and pit the cherries (or prepare the other fruit if using an alternative). In a large glass jar or airtight container, place the fruit and add the sugar and citrus zest.

2. If using spices, add them to the jar. You might use a couple of cloves or a cinnamon stick for added flavor.

3. Pour the brandy or white wine over the fruit and spices in the jar.

4. Seal the jar tightly and place it in a cool, dark place for about a month or more. Ensure the jar is sealed properly to prevent evaporation.

5. Shake the jar gently every few days to mix the ingredients. After a month or longer, strain the mixture through a fine mesh sieve or cheesecloth to remove the fruit and spices. Bottle the resulting liquid into clean, airtight containers.

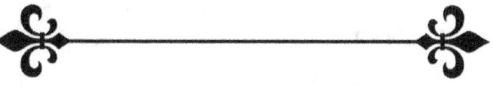

Chapter Ten

Setting the Table
Decoding the Ambiance of an Imperial Banquet

As whispers of political intrigue reverberated through ornate ballrooms and corridors of regal palaces, Napoleon, a man of towering ambition and discerning tastes, left an indelible mark not only on the maps of Europe but also on the tables where treaties were forged and alliances sealed. Within the confines of the Tuileries Palace and Malmaison, his favored residences, the table was a stage for culinary diplomacy and showmanship. In the opulence of his court, elaborate banquets unfolded, showcasing the finest culinary creations and the most exquisite wines, a testament to his appreciation for the artistry of fine dining.

The integral player in any Napoleonic era soirée was the palpable character of the event itself. From the elegance of table settings adorned with ornate silverware and fine porcelain to the regal atmosphere crafted by flickering candlelight and the strains of classical music, every detail played a role in elevating a meal to an experience worthy of an emperor. Recreating the atmosphere of lavish refinement involves the flavors on the plate and their presentation. The ambiance was a mesmerizing interplay of silks and brocades, gilded candelabras casting a warm glow upon the assembled magnificence, and the heady aroma of exotic perfumes mingling with the tantalizing scents emanating from the kitchens.

In the glittering halls of the court, where elegance and decorum danced hand in hand, the art of entertaining became a symphony of refinement and grace. To host a feast fit for a legend was not merely a culinary endeavor but a meticulous choreography of manners, ritual, and refined conversation. Etiquette reigned supreme at Napoleon's gatherings, dictating the rhythm of the evening. From the subtle inclinations of the head to how cutlery met porcelain, every movement spoke volumes about one's social standing. The rules of engagement extended beyond the dining table, encompassing the art of tête-à-tête, where wit and erudition were prized, and the skillful navigation of topics was a testament to one's intellect and sophistication.

Music played a pivotal role in the grandeur and ambiance of feasts, enhancing the sensory experience and underscoring the grandiosity of the event. Melodies danced through the air, setting the tone and rhythm for the evening's indulgence. It was not merely background noise but an essential entertainment element, setting the tone for different parts of the feast, from guests' arrival to the meal's climax. Composers and musicians of the time were often commissioned to create specific pieces or arrangements tailored for these occasions, showcasing the prowess of the court and adding an extra layer of sophistication. Whether it was the stirring sounds of brass fanfare signaling the commencement of the feast or the soft tones that accompanied the courses, music was a language of prestige, refinement, and cultural expression that raised the entire dining experience to a realm of majestic indulgence.

Seating arrangements were crafted with precision, considering not only the hierarchy of guests but also the dynamics that would foster engaging interaction. The role of the host transcended mere hospitality; it was a performance in itself. Guiding guests through the evening, striking the perfect balance between warmth and formality, and ensuring that each person felt valued and engaged were hallmarks of a successful host. The art of conversation flowed effortlessly, embracing diverse topics that sparked intellectual stimulation and camaraderie among guests. Pacing the meal was artful, allowing guests to savor each course without feeling rushed. It was a symphony of timing, where the crescendo of flavors unfolded gradually, building anticipation and culminating in a grand finale that left an indelible mark on the palate.

The meal's pacing was an art form and cornerstone of the Napoleonic dining experience. The progression of courses, from *hors d'oeuvres* to the *pièce de résistance,* the grand finale of desserts, followed a cadence that ensured a harmonious flow, each dish building upon the previous one to create a pinnacle of flavors. Each course was presented with finesse on elegant porcelain accompanied by ornate silverware, and the finest wines and spirits were carefully selected to enhance the gastronomic journey. Service, too, was a performance—an intricate ballet of precision and grace. Each dish was elegant, reflecting the attention to detail and craftsmanship that defined the emperor's feasts.

Recreating a Napoleonic Era Gala can be an elaborate and immersive experience. Here are some steps to help you organize such an event.

Setting the Scene

Venue: Choose a location that resembles the ambiance of the Napoleonic era. A historic mansion or grand ballroom would work well, as would a location with architectural elements reminiscent of the period. A venue with gardens or outdoor spaces could host activities like dancing or leisurely walks.

Décor: Incorporate ornate details such as gilded mirrors, elaborate centerpieces, damask or brocade fabrics, and period-specific art pieces. Consider using colors popular during that time, such as rich reds, blues, and golds.

Music: Live music is vital. Hire musicians or an ensemble to play classical music from the Napoleonic era, like Mozart, Beethoven, and Haydn, or Napoleon's personal favorite, Italian composer, Giovanni Paisiello. Consider a string quartet or a harpsichord player.

Dress Code

Attire: Encourage guests to wear attire typical of the period. This includes tailcoats, waistcoats, breeches, and cravats for men. Women could wear empire-waist gowns, gloves, and intricate hairstyles with feathers or ribbons.

Guidance: Provide a dress code guide or examples to help guests with their attire. Collaborate with a costume designer or local theater group to help guests with their attire or offer costume rentals.

Entertainment

Dance: Arrange for instructors to teach guests popular dances of the time, such as the waltz, quadrille, or minuet.

Parlor Games: Include period-appropriate games (whist, faro), fortune-telling, or other parlor games (charades) to entertain guests.

Food and Drinks

Menu: Use this book as a starting point for savory inspiration. Consult a historical chef or caterer to create the perfect menu that incorporates French, Italian, and other European dishes that were popular during that time.

Beverages: Offer wines, brandies, and champagne, but remember also to offer non-alcoholic options like fruit punches or flavored syrups.

Ambiance and Details

Candlelight: Use candles and candelabras for lighting to replicate the era's ambiance.

Attention to Detail: Pay attention to small details like table settings (silverware, china, and glassware), napkin folds, and floral arrangements, keeping them in line with the historical period.

Host Interaction: Encourage hosts or hired actors to interact with guests, portraying historical figures or characters from the era.

Invitations and Communication

Invitations: Design invitations that reflect the elegance and style of the period, using calligraphy, wax seals, and artistic motifs from the era. Ensure the invitations clearly outline the dress code and expectations for the evening.

Communication: Use language and etiquette reminiscent of the Napoleonic era in your communication leading up to the event to set the tone for guests.

Remember, attention to detail will significantly enhance the authenticity and enjoyment of your Napoleonic Era Banquet. Guests will appreciate the effort you put into creating an immersive experience!

Gastronomic Diplomacy: Napoleon's Culinary Relations

Historically, diplomacy has been shaped by a myriad of strategies and tools, some conventional and others more unexpected. One of the most intriguing and delectable facets of such maneuvering emerged during an era when the fate of nations hung on the balance of power and the subtleties of statecraft: the age of Napoleon. At the heart of his foreign policy playbook lay an unexpected yet profoundly influential element—gastronomy. From lavish feasts that dazzled dignitaries to carefully orchestrated banquets designed to sway the tides of negotiation, Napoleon astutely understood the intimate connection between dining and his desire for global hegemony.

The influence of French gastronomy extended far beyond the borders of the nation. Across Europe, French culinary practices were admired and emulated, becoming a symbol of refinement and taste. French chefs and their techniques found their way into the courts of neighboring countries, where nobility sought to replicate the sophistication of French dining. Napoleon understood that the flavors and customs of the table could serve as bridges between nations, fostering camaraderie and smoothing the rough edges of international relations by shaping perceptions and promoting goodwill. Lavish banquets hosted in his courts were not just feasts but carefully orchestrated diplomatic maneuvers to solidify alliances and project French culinary prestige onto the world stage. Every detail, from the selection of dishes to the seating arrangement, was meticulously crafted to convey messages, solidify alliances, or assert dominance. The dinner table became a stage where diplomacy developed amidst the clinking of glasses and the savored aromas of exquisite dishes.

Foreign leaders were often greeted with the finest French cuisine, carefully selected to cater to their tastes and preferences. Culinary exchanges became a means of building rapport and relaxing the atmosphere so the nuances of diplomacy could be explored away from the formalities of official meetings. Informal conversations over shared meals often laid the groundwork for formal discussions. The menu became a language where each dish conveyed subtle messages—whether showcasing local specialties to highlight cultural richness or cleverly selecting ingredients to appeal to the palates of visiting dignitaries. The careful arrangement of courses mirrored the strategic alignment of alliances and negotiations.

Napoleon's strategic use of gastronomy elicited varied responses from the public. While some viewed his lavish banquets as symbols of French grandeur and sophistication, others criticized the extravagance amidst economic challenges and societal disparities. Despite this conflict, the impact of Napoleon's gastronomic diplomacy echoes through history, leaving a legacy that transcends his era. Contemporary leaders draw inspiration from Napoleon's playbook, engaging in culinary exchanges, hosting state banquets, and utilizing gastronomy to bridge cultural divides and forge diplomatic ties.

Further Reading:

Nester, William. *Napoleon and the Art of Diplomacy: How War and Hubris Determined the Rise and Fall of the French Empire.* El Dorado Hills, CA: Savas Beatie, 2012.

Chapter Eleven

Rations and Resilience
Military Provisions during the Napoleonic Wars

Amidst the thunderous clash of empires and echoing cannon fire, it is easy to overlook the key to Napoleon's success on the battlefield—the military provisions that fueled the humanity of war. In the face of sweeping vanquishments and strategic maneuvers, combat supplies emerged as silent yet pivotal warriors in their own right. From the frigid reaches of Russia to the sunbaked fields of Spain, the Napoleonic Wars, with their political upheavals and theatrics, were more than a clash of armies; they were a crucible where logistics, resourcefulness, and resilience were tested with every meal distributed, every grain conserved, and every creative adaptation made amidst scarcity.

Behind the grandeur of Napoleon's conquests lay a complex network of farms, markets, wagons, and ships - an infrastructure crucial for sustaining his forces. This journey traversed geographic landscapes and cultural realms, revealing the convergence of necessity and innovation that shaped the culinary battleground across continents and empires. It is also the human narratives entwined within the supply chains - the stories of farmers toiling the fields, merchants navigating perilous routes, soldiers relying on daily rations, and the logistical personnel orchestrating sustenance movement across war-torn landscapes. Collectively, these stories, often overshadowed by tales of military prowess, offer depth to a subject usually defined by the machinery of war alone.

Anatomy of a War Machine: The Logistics of Sustaining Armies

In the grand theatre of war, where generals plotted strategies and battles roared, the logistics of feeding armies emerged as an intricate and formidable challenge. Providing sustenance to soldiers traversing vast terrains and enduring harsh climates was a management puzzle that demanded meticulous planning and constant adaptation to orchestrate. Feeding his army of hundreds of thousands demanded an unprecedented organization of resources. Food, fodder for horses, ammunition, and other supplies had to be consistently delivered to the frontlines, often spanning thousands of miles across hostile territories.

The success or failure of battles often hung on the availability of supplies. Instances abound where Napoleon's forces, despite tactical superiority, were weakened or thwarted due to inadequate provisions. The retreat from Moscow is a stark reminder of the catastrophic consequences of insufficient logistical support. Soldiers often faced reduced rations, leading to morale issues and diminished combat efficiency. Yet, amidst scarcity came remarkable displays of ingenuity - foraging, trading with locals, and adapting to alternative food sources to sustain the troops.

From Field to Frontline: Agricultural Mobilization

Napoleonic Europe thrived on its agrarian societies, where the toil of farmers and peasants sustained not only populations but also the grand ambitions of emperors and generals. However, the landscape of agriculture underwent a seismic shift as the demands of war challenged the very foundation of rural life, and the demands of conflict shattered the tranquility of the countryside. Typically untouched by the politics of distant capitals, planters were embroiled in the chaos of empire-building. Their fields, once sources of self-sustenance, became arenas for meeting the escalating demands for provisions for armies in distant battles.

Farmers were forced to innovate under the weight of unprecedented demands. The pressure for increased yield spurred the adoption of new techniques - crop rotation, selective breeding, and the introduction of previously unknown crops. These changes were born from necessity, driven by the imperative to meet the ever-growing need for sustenance. With men conscripted into military service, societal roles were altered as women assumed pivotal functions in agricultural production. Their contributions in tilling fields, harvesting crops, and managing farms became indispensable, ensuring the continuity of agrarian output amidst the turmoil of war.

The Crucial Link: The Quartermaster in the Napoleonic Wars

Transporting provisions across vast distances to sustain armies was an intricate dance of logistics during the Napoleonic era. The success or failure of military campaigns hinged on the efficiency of moving food, fodder, and supplies to the frontlines. At the heart of the vital supply line were the personnel whose responsibilities were multidimensional and crucial for ensuring that troops were adequately provisioned, which was essential for maintaining morale, readiness, and effectiveness in combat.

The quartermaster was the linchpin in this daunting odyssey. Their many functions included:

- *Supply Planning*: He was responsible for planning and organizing the distribution of supplies, including food, ammunition, clothing, equipment, and other essentials needed by the troops. They had to anticipate the army's needs based on factors like unit movements, weather conditions, and the duration of campaigns.

- *Resource Allocation*: They allocated resources based on priorities, ensuring that the frontline received the necessary supplies, which involved balancing limited resources to meet the varied needs of different units within the army. Logistical personnel had to navigate the delicate balance between scarcity and surplus. Scarcity led to rationing, impacting troop morale and combat effectiveness. Surplus, while seemingly beneficial, posed challenges of storage and preservation, often resulting in wastage.

- *Acquisition of Supplies*: Quartermasters were tasked with procuring supplies from various sources, including purchasing, requisitioning, or foraging. They had to establish routes, negotiate with providers, and manage inventories to maintain adequate stocks. This task grew harder as shortages ensued and profiteering and black markets grew, causing exorbitant prices for civilians and soldiers alike.

- *Inventory Management*: They oversaw inventory levels, tracked the quantities of provisions and equipment available, and kept records of stockpiles to avoid shortages or overstocking. Once supplies were received, the quartermaster organized their distribution to units in the field. Establishing supply lines across vast territories, often through hostile regions, was a logistical nightmare. Roads, bridges, and waterways had to be secured and properly maintained to ensure the smooth passage of resources. Innovative strategies were employed to protect convoys from ambushes and raids by enemy forces and bandits.

- *Transport Logistics*: Wagons, meticulously organized into convoys, traversed challenging terrains while ships navigated perilous waters to ensure a steady supply of provisions. Pack animals, essential for mobility in rugged landscapes, were pivotal in transporting goods to inaccessible areas.

It was a daunting job under normal conditions. Still, battlefield quartermasters also had to adapt to changing circumstances, such as disrupted supply lines due to battles, inclement weather, or the unpredictability of war. They often had to improvise and find alternative means to meet the army's needs. Additionally, handling perishable supplies, managing spoilage, and mitigating risks associated with theft, rot, or damage during transportation were constant challenges that required meticulous planning and risk management. Any disruptions could negatively impact troop morale and combat readiness. A competent quartermaster was worth their weight in gold.

Supplying the Troops: Rations, Scarcity, and Subsistence

According to Napoleon, "Five things there are from which the soldier must never be separated: his gun, his cartridges, his field pack, his rations for at least four days, and his digging tool."[3] He understood that the lifeblood of any army lay in the provision of rations—the sustenance that filled the soldiers' bodies and spirits. They were not mere meals; they were the bedrock upon which the effectiveness and morale of troops rested. Soldiers typically received a daily or weekly ration based on rank and the unit's resources. However, the availability and quality fluctuated significantly based on logistical successes or failures.

Staple carbohydrates form a significant portion of rations. Soldiers often received durable hardtack biscuits or bread, which could last for extended periods without spoiling. These were typically the primary source of calories for troops. Salted beef or pork, sometimes supplemented with preserved meats, formed another essential part of rations. These provisions were served with salt to extend their shelf life and were crucial for protein intake. Dried peas, beans, lentils, or rice were often included to provide additional nutrients and variety. Onions, garlic, and other root vegetables were occasionally given to soldiers, as would supplements like salt, vinegar, or dried fruits.

Shortages of provisions were commonplace. Soldiers often faced reduced rations, leading to hunger and discontent among the ranks. Deprivation of sustenance resulted in a demoralized army. Hunger, fatigue, and physical weakness eroded the soldiers' morale, affecting their ability to endure the rigors of battle. Moreover, insubordination and desertion increased as a result during severe periods. In lean times, soldiers resorted to innovative methods to supplement their rations. Foraging for wild edibles, trading with locals, and hunting became essential survival tactics, ensuring a degree of subsistence amidst deprivation.

During the Napoleonic Wars, soldiers' mealtimes and the rituals surrounding them formed essential facets of their daily routines, offering moments of respite during the chaos of warfare. While chow was typically scheduled, times could vary depending on circumstances such as active engagement, marching, or strategic movements. Soldiers often had to adapt their eating schedules to fit the exigencies of warfare. Regardless of the actual timing, meals provided opportunities for troops to gather, fostering a sense of kinship and shared experiences, often through sharing stories, singing songs, or observing customs that added a sense of familiarity to their lives. Indeed, mealtimes were psychological anchors crucial for maintaining morale and camaraderie, providing soldiers with a semblance of normalcy and comfort amid uncertainty.

Legacy and Lessons Learned

Despite the turmoil, the era heralded lasting changes that revolutionized warfare logistics. It emphasized the indispensability of well-organized and efficient support and transportation networks and the profound impact of provisions on the outcomes of conflicts. The ration system laid the groundwork for modern military administration. It highlighted the importance of an adequate supply chain, adaptable cooking methods, and ensuring sufficient and balanced nutrition to troops in wartime conditions. The tales of scarcity, innovation, and endurance underscore the human capacity for resilience amidst adversity. These narratives offer timeless lessons in adapting to challenges, fostering camaraderie, and displaying unwavering resolve in dire circumstances. Napoleon's campaigns exemplify how the supply chain was the silent partner to victories, an unsung hero whose significance echoes through the ages.

Further Reading:
Crowdy, Terry. *Napoleon's Infantry Handbook*. Barnsley, England: Pen & Sword Books, 2015.

Hardtack Biscuits

Ingredients

- 4 cups of flour
- 1 cup of water
- Pinch of salt

Instructions

1. Preheat the oven to 375°F (190°C).

2. Mix the flour and salt in a bowl, gradually adding water to form a stiff dough.

3. Roll out the dough to about 1/4 inch thickness and cut into squares or circles.

4. Place the pieces on a baking sheet and bake for about 30 minutes or until dry and hard.

5. Let the biscuits cool completely before storing them in airtight containers. These biscuits can last for weeks or months and were a staple in soldiers' rations.

Beef Jerky

Ingredients

- 2 lbs (900g) of lean beef, thinly sliced
- 1/2 cup soy sauce
- 1/4 cup Worcestershire sauce
- 2 tablespoons brown sugar
- 1 teaspoon black pepper
- 1 teaspoon garlic powder
- 1 teaspoon onion powder

Instructions

1. Mix soy sauce, Worcestershire sauce, brown sugar, black pepper, garlic powder, and onion powder in a bowl.

2. Add the thinly sliced beef to the marinade, ensuring the beef is coated evenly. Marinate for at least 4 hours or overnight in the refrigerator.

3. Preheat the oven to 175°F (80°C) or use a food dehydrator.

4. Place the marinated beef strips on a baking sheet or dehydrator trays.

5. Bake or dehydrate for 4-6 hours until the beef is dried and firm. Let it cool completely before storing in airtight containers.

Portable Soup

Ingredients

- 2 lbs (900g) beef or chicken bones
- 2 onions, chopped
- 2 carrots, chopped
- 2 celery stalks, chopped
- Salt and pepper to taste

Instructions

1. Simmer bones, vegetables, salt, and pepper in a large pot of water for several hours until the liquid reduces significantly.

2. Strain the liquid and discard the solids.

3. Pour the strained liquid onto a baking sheet and allow it to cool and solidify.

4. Cut the solidified broth into small squares or rectangles.

5. Wrap these squares in cloth or wax paper and store them in airtight containers. Soldiers could carry these 'portable soups' and reconstitute them by adding hot water to make a nourishing broth.

Officer's Stew

Ingredients

- 2 lbs (900g) beef or venison, cubed
- 2 onions, chopped
- 4-5 potatoes, diced
- 2 carrots, sliced
- 2 cups beef broth
- Salt, pepper, and dried herbs to taste
- Olive oil or fat for cooking

Instructions

1. Heat oil or fat in a pot over medium heat. Add the onions and meat, cooking until browned.

2. Add potatoes, carrots, beef broth, salt, pepper, and herbs.

3. Bring to a boil, then reduce heat and simmer for about an hour or until the meat is tender and the vegetables are cooked.

4. Adjust seasoning as needed. This stew provided officers with a hearty and nourishing meal during campaigns.

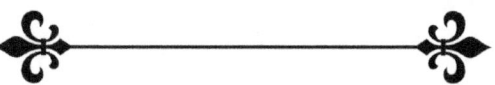

Pea Soup

Ingredients

- 1 cup dried split peas
- 1 onion, chopped
- 2-3 carrots, diced
- 2-3 potatoes, diced
- Salt and pepper to taste
- Water or broth

Instructions

1. Rinse the split peas and place them in a pot with enough water or broth to cover them by an inch.

2. Add chopped onion, carrots, and potatoes to the pot.

3. Bring to a boil, then reduce heat and simmer for 1-2 hours until the peas are tender and the soup thickens.

4. Season with salt and pepper to taste. This soup provided a hearty and nutritious meal for soldiers.

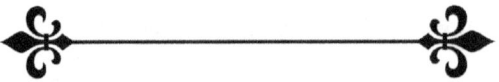

Soldier's Stew

Ingredients

- 1 lb (450g) salt pork, diced
- 2 onions, chopped
- 2-3 potatoes, diced
- 2 cups dried beans (such as navy beans), soaked overnight
- Salt, pepper, and dried herbs to taste
- Water

Instructions

1. In a large pot, fry the diced salt pork until browned. Remove excess fat if desired.

2. Add chopped onions and sauté until translucent.

3. Drain and rinse the soaked beans, then add them to the pot along with potatoes, salt, pepper, herbs, and enough water to cover the ingredients.

4. Bring to a boil, then reduce heat and simmer for 1-2 hours until the beans are tender and the stew thickens. Adjust seasoning if needed.

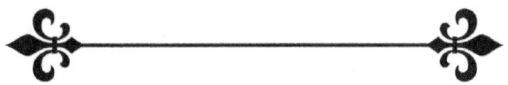

Bannock Bread

Ingredients

- 2 cups flour
- 1 tablespoon baking powder
- 1/2 teaspoon salt
- Water or milk

Instructions

1. Mix flour, baking powder, and salt in a bowl.

2. Gradually add water or milk, mixing until a dough forms.

3. Knead the dough on a floured surface for a few minutes.

4. Flatten the dough into a round shape, about 1/2 inch thick.

5. Cook the bannock on a hot, greased skillet or over an open flame for about 5-7 minutes on each side until golden brown and cooked through. This bread provided a portable and hearty staple for soldiers.

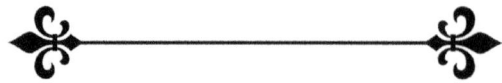

Chapter Twelve

Conquest at the Table
Influences from Annexed Territories

Before the dawn of the Napoleonic era, Europe was a patchwork of diverse culinary traditions, each region boasting its unique flavors, ingredients, and cooking techniques. It was a mosaic of diverse cuisines, each bearing the distinct imprint of its country's history, traditions, and natural bounty. While the French Revolution had already set the stage for social upheaval and cultural evolution, it was under the visionary leadership of Napoleon that Europe experienced a savory metamorphosis like never before. As military campaigns conquered vast swathes of Europe, from Italy to the Low Countries, from Spain to parts of Germany, each annexed territory brought a tempting array of previously unknown or unexplored influences to the French table. Indeed, it was not just a clash of nations but also kitchens that left an indelible mark on the evolution of European cuisine.

ITALY

Napoleon's conquests in Italy during the late 18th century marked a pivotal phase in his early military career and a significant chapter in European history. His campaigns, characterized by strategic brilliance and tactical innovation, reshaped the geopolitical landscape of the peninsula. The Italian campaign of 1796-1797 displayed his audacious maneuvers and decisive victories against the Austrian forces, showcasing his genius and cementing his reputation as a formidable commander. His triumphs at battles like Lodi and Arcola allowed him to secure key territories, dismantle longstanding power structures, and establish client republics sympathetic to French interests. These campaigns demonstrated his military prowess and laid the groundwork for his future ambitions, propelling him to greater heights on the European stage.

The general's forays into Italy exposed him to aromas and tastes beyond his Corsican heritage that would forever alter the landscape of French cuisine. The simplicity and elegance of Italian dishes captivated the emperor's palate. Staples like tomatoes, olive oil, garlic, basil, pasta, and risotto found their way into the larders of French kitchens, introducing a whole new variety of flavors and vehicles to the established culinary repertoire. Once exotic and novel, these ingredients soon became integral to French cooking. The luscious tomatoes brightened sauces and stews, while fragrant olive oil lent its golden hue and distinctive taste to dishes that had previously relied on butter. Garlic and basil added depth and complexity, weaving into sauces, soups, and marinades. Pasta, in its myriad of shapes and forms, captured the imagination of chefs, and risotto became a canvas for experimentation with its creamy allure and ability to absorb flavors. Italian influence did not stop at main courses; they also extended into desserts and wines. Tiramisu, cannoli, and panna cotta metamorphosed in French kitchens, adopting new nuances and adornments. At the same time, the allure of Italian wines, from the bold Chianti of Tuscany to the crisp whites of Piedmont, found their way onto French tables, offering a spectrum of flavors and aromas previously unexplored.

EGYPT

As the 18th century drew to a close, eager to expand his empire and influence, Napoleon set his sights on Egypt, envisioning a strategic route to challenge British trade dominance and assert France's global power. Conquests in Egypt marked a pivotal chapter in his military career and pursuit of international influence. His campaign was a mix of military triumphs and cultural exploration, notably by the Battle of the Pyramids and the capture of Cairo. Despite initial successes, the venture faced significant challenges, including the British naval victory at the Battle of the Nile and the emergence of local uprisings. The campaign ultimately faltered, leading to his departure in 1799. However, this endeavor sparked immense curiosity about Egypt in Europe, fueling a wave of Egyptomania and contributing to significant advancements in archaeology, history, and the study of ancient Egyptian culture.

Amidst the tumult, a silent exchange was underway. French soldiers marveled at the diversity of previously unknown ingredients such as coriander, cumin, cardamom, and mint that teased their palates. At the same time, figs, dates, and eggplants introduced new dimensions to their culinary imagination. After Napoleon's expedition to Egypt, French cuisine transformed remarkably, embracing these new influences, and the once-unfamiliar flavors were seamlessly integrated into classic recipes that delighted and expanded culinary boundaries. Meats, poultry, and seafood marinated and cooked with new exotic spice blends produced aromatic tajines, succulent roasts, and innovative dishes.

AUSTRIA

Napoleon's conquests in Austria were pivotal to his ambitious pursuit of European dominance. During the early 19th century, his military brilliance and strategic maneuvers proved formidable. In 1805, at the Battle of Austerlitz, also known as the "Battle of the Three Emperors," Napoleon's French forces decisively defeated the combined armies of Austria and Russia, compelling Austria to sign the Treaty of Pressburg, stripping it of significant territories such Venetia and Tyrol. In 1809, the conflict resumed with the War of the Fifth Coalition. Despite initial setbacks, Napoleon emerged victorious after the Battle of Wagram, leading to the Treaty of Schönbrunn. This treaty imposed harsh terms on Austria, resulting in further territorial losses and solidifying French dominance over central Europe.

Nestled in the heart of Europe, Austria boasted a culinary tradition that blended influences from neighboring regions while maintaining its unique character. Its cuisine relied on ingredients like potatoes, cabbage, root vegetables, and grains, forming the basis of comforting dishes such as dumplings, stews, and roasts. Iconic dishes like *wiener schnitzel* (breaded and fried veal or pork cutlet) and *apfelstrudel* (apple strudel) became synonymous with Austrian culinary excellence. Aromatic herbs like marjoram, thyme, and caraway, as well as spices such as paprika and juniper, added depth and complexity to dishes. The union of Napoleon and Archduchess Marie Louise of Austria in 1810 served as more than a political alliance. It was also a gastronomic fusion between the two empires that left a lasting historical impact.

GERMANY

Germany was a cornerstone of Napoleon's military campaigns, reshaping Central Europe's political and territorial landscape. His victories at battles like Austerlitz (1805) and Jena-Auerstedt (1806) showcased his tactical brilliance. They led to the establishment of the Confederation of the Rhine, a coalition of German states under French influence, which allowed Napoleon to exert significant control over the region, influencing alliances and installing rulers loyal to his cause. However, resistance against French domination persisted, culminating in the Sixth Coalition War. The decisive Battle of Leipzig (1813), also known as the Battle of Nations, was a turning point, leading to the eventual collapse of his rule in Germany and his exile to Elba. Napoleon's conquests in Germany showcased his military prowess but also marked the eventual unraveling of his European empire in the face of staunch opposition and shifting ententes.

From hearty stews to delicate pastries, German cuisine reflected the traditions and flavors of its regions. Known for its hearty fare, Bavaria offered dishes like *Schweinshaxe* (roasted pork knuckle) and pretzels, along with the iconic Oktoberfest favorites such as *Weisswurst* and sauerkraut. Franconia celebrated specialties like Nuremberg sausages, gingerbread, and the aromatic *Schäufele* (pork shoulder), showcasing its unique culinary identity. The Rhine Valley introduced dishes like Sauerbraten (marinated pot roast). Rye and wheat formed the basis of German bread. At the same time, potatoes became a staple after their introduction from the Americas, leading to dishes like *Kartoffelsalat* (potato salad) and *Kartoffelsuppe* (potato soup). From succulent bratwurst and liverwurst to smoked ham and the famous schnitzels, meats were central to German cuisine, often prepared through roasting or braising techniques.

SPAIN

Fraught with challenges and resistance, Spain marked a tumultuous chapter in Napoleon's imperial ambitions. His invasion in 1808 aimed to impose his brother, Joseph, as the new ruler, thus ousting the monarchy and securing French interests. However, this move sparked fierce opposition from the native populace, igniting a prolonged and brutal guerrilla war that strained resources and manpower. The Peninsular War (1808-1814), characterized by unconventional maneuvers and relentless Spanish and Portuguese opposition, proved to be a quagmire for Napoleon's forces. Despite early successes, including capturing major cities like Madrid, the constant insurrection and the British intervention under Wellington ultimately led to the erosion of French control in Spain. The campaigns became a draining conflict that highlighted the limits of the empire and an inability to subdue the fervent nationalism and tactics of the Iberian people.

Spanish cuisine was a tapestry woven with Moorish influences, regional specialties, and an array of bold flavors. Paella, iconic and flavored with saffron and brimming with seafood, chicken, or rabbit, reflected the rich diversity of Spanish ingredients. Gazpacho, a refreshing Andalusian cold soup made with tomatoes, peppers, cucumbers, and garlic, offered a taste of the Mediterranean sunshine. *Jamón ibérico*, prized cured ham derived from Iberian pigs, showcased Spain's mastery of charcuterie. The tradition of tapas, small, flavorful dishes meant for sharing, captured the essence of Spanish conviviality and featured an array of flavors, from olives and almonds to chorizo and seafood. Spanning coastlines, Spain celebrated various seafood dishes, from simple grilled sardines to complex fish stews like the Catalan zarzuela. These tastes captivated the French and sowed the seeds of fusion between neighbors.

THE LOW COUNTRIES

Campaigns in this region (comprising present-day Belgium, Luxembourg, and parts of the Netherlands), particularly during the late 18th and early 19th centuries, were strategic moves aimed at consolidating territories and ensuring a buffer against British power. Through victories like Austerlitz and Jena-Auerstedt, Napoleon extended French dominance into the Low Countries, creating the Kingdom of Holland under his brother Louis Bonaparte's rule. However, resistance to French rule persisted among the local populace, and he faced continuous challenges to maintain control. Ultimately, his defeat at the Battle of Waterloo (1815), where British and Prussian forces decisively ended his rule, marked the conclusion of his conquests in the Low Countries and signaled the end of his reign as emperor of the French.

Belgium's culinary identity featured iconic dishes like *moules-frites* (mussels and fries), *carbonnade flamande* (beef and beer stew), and waffles, showcasing the country's diverse flavors. It was also renowned for chocolate craftsmanship, and pralines became synonymous with indulgence and artistry, elevating its reputation as a chocolatier. Dutch cuisine highlighted herring, cheese, and indulgent treats like stroopwafels (syrup waffles) and *oliebollen* (deep-fried dough balls). The Netherlands' colonial history brought Indonesian spices that enhanced culinary offerings with exotic tastes. Cheeses like Gouda and Edam showcased the Dutch dairy heritage.

EASTERN EUROPE

Military triumphs and complex political maneuvering marked Napoleon's forrays in Eastern Europe. His campaigns in the region disrupted established power structures. Victories in battles like Friedland (1807) led to treaties that reshaped the area, such as the Treaty of Tilsit, where Russia and France allied. Napoleon aimed to exert control over Poland and weaken Russian influence in the region through these alliances. However, his ambitions faced challenges, notably during the disastrous invasion of Russia (1812), where harsh weather and resistance led to significant losses for the Grande Armée. The campaign's legacy reverberates as a cautionary tale of the perils of overextension and underestimating the challenges of warfare in unfamiliar terrain and hostile climates. Napoleon sought to impose French hegemony, redraw territorial boundaries, and install puppet governments in Eastern Europe, yet faced fierce resistance from local powers and sparked nationalist fervor, ultimately contributing to the erosion of his control in the region.

Eastern European cuisine celebrated a rich and diverse array of dishes. Poland tables featured pierogi (filled dumplings), hearty soups like borscht, and flavorful dishes such as *golabki* (cabbage rolls), reflecting a mix of Slavic and Central European influences. Hungary's cuisine highlighted goulash, *paprikash* (dishes flavored with paprika), and the indulgent Dobos torte. Czechia and Slovakia celebrated dishes like *svíčková* (beef with cream sauce), *koláče* (pastries), and *halušky* (dumplings), emphasizing comfort food and simple yet satisfying flavors. Russia boasted beef stroganoff and caviar. Eastern European cuisine relied on staples like potatoes, cabbage, grains, and root vegetables, used sour cream, dill, and other distinctive ingredients, and relied on techniques such as pickling and fermenting developed out of necessity to survive harsh winters in the region.

SCANDINAVIA

Napoleon's involvement in Scandinavia was limited compared to his engagements in other parts of Europe. His efforts in the region primarily revolved around diplomatic maneuvering and attempts to secure alliances rather than direct conquest. Through the Treaty of Tilsit (1807), Napoleon sought to involve Denmark-Norway in his Continental System, a blockade to isolate British trade. This led to Britain's bombardment of Copenhagen (1807). Despite his ambitions to influence Scandinavia, Napoleon's involvement remained primarily diplomatic, with limited direct military engagements in the region.

Encompassing the countries of Sweden, Norway, Denmark, and Finland, Scandinavia boasted cuisine celebrating a blend of rustic simplicity and regional specialties. Sweden's kitchens featured iconic dishes like meatballs, gravlax (cured salmon), and lingongerry jam, showcasing a balance of hearty flavors and delicate preserves. Norway's maritime influence led to a focus on seafood, with dishes like *rakfisk* (fermented fish) and *klippfisk* (dried and salted cod) reflecting its coastal traditions. Denmark's chefs crafted *smørrebrød* (open-faced sandwiches), *flæskesteg* (roast pork), and the beloved Danish pastries, emphasizing simplicity and quality ingredients. Berries, mushrooms, and wild herbs were integral to Scandinavian cooking, emphasizing a connection to nature and the seasons. Traditional methods, like smoking, salting, and pickling, ensured a year-round food supply.

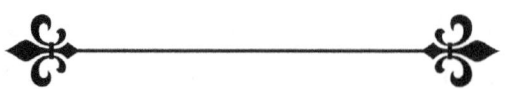

The Napoleonic Era is a testament to more than mere military conquests; it marks a culinary metamorphosis that shaped Europe's diverse flavors and gastronomic heritage. The exchange of culinary traditions from annexed territories during this period brought about a fusion that transcended borders, reshaped the culinary landscape, and left an enduring legacy. The amalgamation of classic French cuisine with new influences such as Italian risotto, Belgian chocolate, German sausages, and Spanish paella, to name a few, transformed recipes and culinary identities. This fusion was not merely a co-opting of ingredients and dishes but a celebration of diversity, a cultural symphony that harmonized regional nuances into a mélange of delectable flavors we continue to enjoy.

Further Reading:

Esdaile, Charles J. *Napoleon's Wars: An International History, 1803-1815.* New York: Viking, 2008.

Spaghetti aux Crevettes à la Provençale

Embark on a culinary voyage to the sun-drenched shores of Provence with Spaghetti aux Crevettes à la Provençale. Inspired by the Mediterranean coast's rustic charm and vibrant flavors, this dish marries succulent shrimp with the fragrant herbs and bold flavors typical of Provençal cuisine.

Ingredients

- 8 ounces (225g) spaghetti
- 1 pound (450g) large shrimp, peeled and deveined
- 3 tablespoons olive oil
- 4 cloves garlic, minced
- 1 pint (about 2 cups) cherry tomatoes, halved
- 1/2 cup pitted black olives, sliced
- 1/4 cup dry white wine (optional)
- 1 tablespoon fresh lemon juice

- 1 teaspoon Herbes de Provence
- Salt and black pepper, to taste
- Crushed red pepper flakes (optional)
- Fresh parsley, chopped, for garnish
- Grated Parmesan cheese, for serving (optional)

Instructions

1. Cook the spaghetti according to the package instructions in a pot of salted boiling water until al dente. Drain and set aside, reserving some pasta water.

2. In a large skillet, heat 2 tablespoons of olive oil over medium heat. Add the shrimp and cook for 2-3 minutes on each side until pink and cooked through. Remove the shrimp from the skillet and set aside.

3. In the same skillet, add the remaining tablespoon of olive oil. Add the minced garlic and cook for about 30 seconds until fragrant, being careful not to burn it.

4. Add the halved cherry tomatoes and sliced olives to the skillet. Cook for about 4-5 minutes until the tomatoes start to soften and release their juices.

5. If using, pour in the white wine to deglaze the pan, scraping up any browned bits from the bottom. Let it simmer for a minute or two until most of the wine evaporates.

6. Return the cooked shrimp to the skillet. Add the fresh lemon juice and herbes de Provence. Season with salt, black pepper, and crushed red pepper flakes, if desired. Stir to combine and let it simmer for a couple of minutes.

7. Add the cooked spaghetti to the skillet and toss everything together, adding a splash of reserved pasta water if needed to loosen the sauce and coat the pasta evenly. Taste and adjust the seasoning if necessary.

8. Garnish the Spaghetti aux Crevettes à la Provençale with chopped fresh parsley. Serve hot, optionally with grated Parmesan cheese on top.

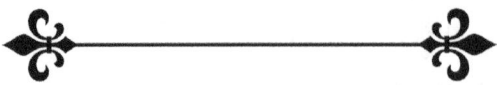

Risotto aux Champignons

Indulge in exquisite flavors with this delightful Risotto aux Champignons recipe. It combines the rich heritage of Italian risotto with a touch of French infusion, creating a dish that captivates the palate and imagination. Earthy mushrooms, lovingly sautéed to perfection, mingle with creamy Arborio rice, creating a velvety texture that melts in your mouth. Enhanced with a hint of aromatic garlic, shallots, and fresh thyme, each spoonful unfolds layers of savory indulgence.

Ingredients

- 1 1/2 cups Arborio rice
- 4 cups chicken or vegetable broth
- 1/2 cup dry white wine
- 1/2 ounce dried wild mushrooms (such as porcini, morels, or chanterelles)
- 2 tablespoons unsalted butter
- 2 tablespoons olive oil
- 1 small onion, finely chopped
- 2 cloves garlic, minced
- 1/2 pound (about 225g) fresh wild mushrooms (such as shiitake, oyster, or cremini), cleaned and sliced
- 1/2 cup grated Parmesan cheese
- Salt and black pepper, to taste
- Chopped fresh parsley for garnish

Instructions

1. In a medium bowl, pour boiling water over the dried wild mushrooms to rehydrate them. Let them soak for about 20-30 minutes until softened. Once rehydrated, drain the mushrooms, reserving the soaking liquid. Chop the rehydrated mushrooms into small pieces.

2. In a saucepan, heat the chicken or vegetable broth over low heat and keep it warm.

3. In a large skillet or sauté pan, heat the olive oil and butter over medium heat. Add

the chopped onion and cook until softened and translucent, about 3-4 minutes. Add the minced garlic and cook for an additional minute until fragrant.

4. Add the fresh sliced wild mushrooms to the skillet and cook until they release their moisture and become tender, about 5-7 minutes.

5. Stir in the rehydrated wild mushrooms and Arborio rice. Cook for 1-2 minutes, stirring constantly, until the rice is well-coated with the oil and mushrooms.

6. Pour in the white wine and cook, stirring constantly, until the wine has been absorbed by the rice.

7. Begin adding the warm chicken or vegetable broth to the rice mixture, one ladleful at a time, stirring constantly and allowing each addition to be absorbed before adding more. Continue this process until the rice is creamy and tender but still slightly firm to the bite (al dente), about 18-20 minutes.

8. Once the risotto reaches the desired consistency, stir in the grated Parmesan cheese until melted and well combined. Season with salt and black pepper to taste.

9. Remove the risotto from the heat and let it rest for a minute or two.

10. To serve, divide the risotto among serving plates or bowls. Garnish with chopped fresh parsley and an extra sprinkle of Parmesan cheese, if desired.

Éclair alla Cannoli

Experience the delightful fusion of French éclair elegance with the timeless charm of Sicilian cannoli in this Éclair alla Cannoli recipe. This indulgent creation marries the lightness of choux pastry with the rich creaminess of cannoli filling, resulting in a decadent treat that tantalizes the taste buds. Each delicate éclair shell, filled with a luscious blend of ricotta cheese, chocolate chips, and hints of citrus zest, promises a symphony of textures and flavors that are a harmonious union of French sophistication and Sicilian indulgence.

Ingredients

For the Choux Pastry

- 1/2 cup water
- 1/2 cup whole milk
- 1/2 cup unsalted butter, cut into cubes
- 1 tablespoon granulated sugar
- 1/4 teaspoon salt
- 1 cup all-purpose flour
- 4 large eggs, at room temperature

For the Cannoli Filling

- 1 1/2 cups ricotta cheese, drained
- 1/2 cup powdered sugar (adjust to taste)
- 1 teaspoon vanilla extract
- Zest of 1 orange
- 1/2 cup mini chocolate chips
- Additional powdered sugar for dusting (optional)

Instructions

For the Choux Pastry

1. Preheat your oven to 400°F (200°C). Line a baking sheet with parchment paper or a silicone mat.

2. In a saucepan, combine water, milk, butter, sugar, and salt. Bring it to a gentle boil over medium heat.

3. Remove the saucepan from the heat and quickly stir in the flour using a wooden spoon until a smooth dough forms and pulls away from the sides of the pan.

4. Return the saucepan to low heat and continue stirring the dough for about 1-2 minutes to slightly dry it out. The dough should come together into a ball and leave a thin film on the bottom of the pan.

5. Transfer the dough to a mixing bowl and let it cool for a few minutes.

6. Gradually add the eggs to the dough, one at a time, beating well after each addition, until the dough becomes smooth and glossy.

7. Fill a piping bag fitted with a round tip with the choux pastry dough.

8. Pipe the dough onto the prepared baking sheet, forming eclairs of your desired size and shape, leaving space between them.

9. Bake the eclairs in the preheated oven for 15 minutes. Reduce the oven temperature to 350°F (175°C) and bake for an additional 10-15 minutes or until golden brown and puffed. Avoid opening the oven door while baking to prevent deflating.

10. Once baked, remove the eclairs from the oven and let them cool completely on a wire rack before filling.

For the Cannoli Filling

1. In a mixing bowl, combine the drained ricotta cheese, powdered sugar, vanilla extract, and orange zest. Mix until smooth and well combined.

2. Fold in the mini chocolate chips into the ricotta mixture.

3. Using a piping bag fitted with a small round tip or a ziplock bag with the corner cut off, fill each cooled eclair with the cannoli filling.

4. Optionally, dust the filled eclairs with powdered sugar before serving.

Duck Confit Paella

Elevate your culinary experience with our Duck Confit Paella recipe—a delightful fusion of French sophistication and Spanish vibrancy. Inspired by the rich traditions of both cuisines, this dish marries tender duck confit with the aromatic flavors and vibrant colors of traditional Spanish paella. With each luxurious spoonful of saffron-infused rice, succulent duck, and a medley of vegetables, you'll embark on a gastronomic journey that celebrates the best of both worlds.

Ingredients

- 2 duck confit legs
- 1 1/2 cups Arborio rice
- 4 cups chicken or vegetable broth
- 1 onion, finely chopped
- 3 cloves garlic, minced
- 1 red bell pepper, diced
- 1 yellow bell pepper, diced
- 1 cup frozen peas
- 1 tomato, diced
- 1 teaspoon smoked paprika
- A pinch of saffron threads
- Salt and freshly ground black pepper
- Olive oil

- Lemon wedges for serving
- Chopped parsley for garnish

Instructions

1. Preheat your oven to 350°F (175°C).

2. In a large skillet or paella pan, heat a tablespoon of olive oil over medium heat.

3. Sear the duck confit legs, skin side down, until golden and crisp, about 5-7 minutes. Remove from the pan and set aside.

4. In the same pan, add a little more olive oil if needed, then add the chopped onion, garlic, and bell peppers. Sauté until the vegetables are softened, about 5-7 minutes.

5. Stir in the diced tomato and smoked paprika. Cook for another 2-3 minutes.

6. Add the Arborio rice to the pan, stirring to coat it with the vegetables and spices.

7. Pour in the chicken or vegetable broth and saffron threads, and season with salt and pepper to taste. Stir well to combine.

8. Nestle the seared duck confit legs into the rice mixture, skin side up.

9. Transfer the skillet or paella pan to the preheated oven and bake for 20-25 minutes, or until the rice is tender and most of the liquid is absorbed.

10. During the last 5 minutes of baking, scatter the frozen peas over the paella and return to the oven to heat through.

11. Once done, remove the paella from the oven and let it rest for a few minutes. Garnish with chopped parsley and serve hot, accompanied by lemon wedges for squeezing over the paella.

Bouillabaisse à la Española

Bouillabaisse à la Española is an exquisite dish that takes the rich and fragrant essence of traditional French bouillabaisse and infuses it with Spanish cuisine's vibrant and aromatic notes. Picture a steaming pot filled with an abundance of succulent seafood swimming in a broth that sings with saffron's warmth, paprika's smokiness, and tomatoes' sweetness. Each spoonful celebrates Mediterranean flavors, transporting you to sun-drenched coastal villages where French and Spanish culinary traditions intertwine.

Ingredients

- 1 lb assorted seafood (such as shrimp, mussels, clams, and firm fish fillets like cod or halibut), cleaned and deveined
- 1 onion, finely chopped
- 2 cloves garlic, minced
- 1 fennel bulb, thinly sliced
- 1 red bell pepper, thinly sliced
- 1 yellow bell pepper, thinly sliced
- 1 cup diced tomatoes (fresh or canned)
- 4 cups fish or seafood broth
- 1/2 cup dry white wine
- 2 tablespoons olive oil
- 1 teaspoon saffron threads
- 1 teaspoon smoked paprika
- Salt and pepper to taste
- Fresh parsley, chopped, for garnish
- Crusty bread, for serving

Instructions

1. In a large pot or Dutch oven, heat the olive oil over medium heat. Add the chopped onion and garlic, and sauté until softened and fragrant, about 3-4 minutes.

2. Add the sliced fennel and bell peppers to the pot, and cook until they start to soften, about 5 minutes.

3. Stir in the diced tomatoes, saffron threads, and smoked paprika. Cook for another 2-3 minutes.

4. Pour in the white wine and fish or seafood broth, and bring the mixture to a simmer. Let it simmer for about 10 minutes to allow the flavors to meld together.

5. Season the broth with salt and pepper to taste.

6. Once the broth is seasoned, add the assorted seafood to the pot. Arrange the seafood evenly in the pot, ensuring that it is submerged in the broth.

7. Cover the pot and let the seafood simmer gently in the broth until cooked through. The cooking time will vary depending on the type of seafood used, but it typically takes about 5-7 minutes for shrimp and fish fillets, and 10-12 minutes for mussels and clams. Discard any mussels or clams that do not open.

8. Once the seafood is cooked, taste the broth and adjust the seasoning if necessary.

9. Serve the Bouillabaisse à la Española hot, garnished with chopped parsley, and accompanied by crusty bread for dipping.

Croquetas de Boeuf

Indulge in the savory delights of French-Spanish fusion with Croquetas de Boeuf. These delectable croquettes encapsulate the essence of culinary artistry, marrying tender beef with a velvety béchamel sauce infused with aromatic spices and herbs. Each crispy bite offers a harmonious blend of flavors and textures, evoking memories of cozy bistros and sun-drenched tapas bars.

Ingredients

- 1/2 lb cooked beef, finely shredded or chopped
- 2 tablespoons butter
- 3 tablespoons all-purpose flour
- 1 cup milk
- 1/4 teaspoon nutmeg
- Salt and pepper, to taste
- 1/4 cup finely chopped onion
- 2 cloves garlic, minced
- 1/4 cup finely chopped parsley
- 2 eggs, beaten
- 1 cup breadcrumbs
- Vegetable oil, for frying

Instructions

1. In a saucepan, melt the butter over medium heat. Add the chopped onion and minced garlic, and sauté until softened and fragrant, about 3-4 minutes.

2. Stir in the flour to form a roux. Cook, stirring constantly, for 1-2 minutes until the mixture turns golden brown.

3. Gradually pour in the milk, stirring continuously to prevent lumps from forming. Cook the mixture until thickened and smooth, about 2-3 minutes.

4. Add the shredded beef, nutmeg, salt, pepper, and chopped parsley to the saucepan. Stir well to combine.

5. Cook the mixture for an additional 2-3 minutes, until heated through and well combined. Remove from heat and allow it to cool completely.

6. Once the beef mixture has cooled, shape it into small croquettes, about 2 inches in length.

7. Dip each croquette into the beaten eggs, then roll them in breadcrumbs until evenly coated.

8. In a deep skillet or fryer, heat the vegetable oil to 350°F (175°C). Carefully add the croquettes to the hot oil in batches, frying until golden brown and crispy, about 3-4 minutes per batch.

9. Use a slotted spoon to transfer the cooked croquettes to a paper towel-lined plate to drain excess oil.

10. Serve the Croquetas de Boeuf hot, garnished with additional chopped parsley if desired. Enjoy as a delicious appetizer or snack.

Quiche Basquaise

Inspired by the vibrant flavors and colorful traditions of Basque cuisine, Quiche Basquaise is a delightful quiche that offers a tantalizing fusion of French elegance and Basque zest. Picture a golden crust filled with a symphony of sautéed bell peppers, sweet cherry tomatoes, savory Bayonne ham, and creamy Gruyère cheese, all embraced by a velvety custard. Each slice celebrates the Basque spirit, inviting you to savor the warmth of the Mediterranean sun and the richness of Basque culinary heritage.

Ingredients

For the Crust

- 1 1/4 cups all-purpose flour
- 1/2 cup unsalted butter, cold and cubed
- 1/4 teaspoon salt
- 3-4 tablespoons ice-cold water

For the Filling

- 1 tablespoon olive oil
- 1 onion, finely chopped
- 1 red bell pepper, thinly sliced
- 1 green bell pepper, thinly sliced
- 1 cup cherry tomatoes, halved
- 200g Bayonne ham or prosciutto, diced
- 1 cup grated Gruyère or Emmental cheese
- 4 large eggs
- 1 cup heavy cream
- Salt and black pepper, to taste
- Fresh basil or parsley, for garnish

Instructions

For the Crust

1. In a food processor, combine the flour, cold butter, and salt. Pulse until the mixture resembles coarse crumbs.

2. Gradually add the ice-cold water, one tablespoon at a time, and pulse until the dough comes together.

3. Turn the dough onto a floured surface, knead it briefly, then shape it into a disc. Wrap in plastic wrap and refrigerate for at least 30 minutes.

4. Preheat the oven to 375°F (190°C).

5. Roll out the chilled dough on a floured surface and line a 9-inch tart or quiche pan. Trim the excess dough.

6. Place parchment paper over the crust and fill it with pie weights or dried beans. Blind bake for 15 minutes. Remove the weights and parchment paper, then bake for an additional 5 minutes until lightly golden. Allow to cool.

For the Filling

1. In a skillet, heat the olive oil over medium heat. Sauté the chopped onion until translucent.

2. Add the sliced bell peppers and cook until softened, about 5-7 minutes.

3. In a bowl, whisk together the eggs and heavy cream. Season with salt and black pepper.

4. Spread the sautéed vegetables, cherry tomatoes, diced Bayonne ham or prosciutto, and grated cheese over the pre-baked crust.

5. Pour the egg and cream mixture over the filling.

6. Bake the quiche in the preheated oven for 30-35 minutes or until the center is set and the top is golden brown.

7. Allow the quiche to cool for a few minutes before slicing.

8. Garnish with fresh basil or parsley before serving.

Ratatouille de Pimientos

Experience the harmonious blend of French elegance and Spanish vibrancy with Ratatouille de Pimientos. This delightful dish pays homage to the rich culinary traditions of both cultures, marrying the rustic charm of French ratatouille with the bold flavors of Spanish pimientos. Imagine a medley of colorful bell peppers, tender eggplant, and succulent zucchini simmered in a fragrant tomato-based sauce infused with smoked paprika and aromatic herbs. Each spoonful offers a symphony of flavors and textures, transporting you to sun-kissed Mediterranean landscapes where culinary magic happens.

Ingredients

- 2 red bell peppers, sliced
- 2 yellow bell peppers, sliced
- 1 large eggplant, diced
- 2 zucchinis, sliced
- 2 tomatoes, diced
- 1 onion, thinly sliced
- 3 cloves garlic, minced
- 3 tablespoons olive oil
- 2 tablespoons tomato paste
- 1 teaspoon smoked paprika
- 1 teaspoon dried thyme
- Salt and black pepper, to taste
- Fresh basil or parsley, chopped, for garnish

Instructions

1. Heat 2 tablespoons of olive oil in a large skillet over medium heat. Add the sliced onion and minced garlic. Sauté until the onion is translucent and fragrant, about 3-4 minutes.

2. Add the sliced bell peppers to the skillet. Cook until the peppers are slightly softened, about 5-7 minutes.

3. Push the peppers to one side of the skillet and add the remaining tablespoon of olive oil to the empty side. Add the diced eggplant and zucchini to the skillet. Cook until the vegetables are tender, about 8-10 minutes.

4. Stir in the diced tomatoes, tomato paste, smoked paprika, dried thyme, salt, and black pepper. Mix well to combine all the ingredients.

5. Reduce the heat to low and let the ratatouille simmer for another 10-15 minutes, allowing the flavors to meld together and the sauce to thicken slightly.

6. Taste and adjust the seasoning as needed.

7. Once the vegetables are tender and the flavors are well combined, remove the skillet from the heat.

8. Garnish the Ratatouille de Pimientos with freshly chopped basil or parsley before serving.

9. Serve the ratatouille warm as a side dish, over rice or pasta, or as a topping for crusty bread.

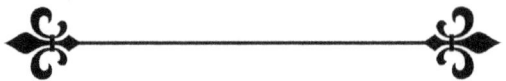

Churros with Dark Chocolate Sauce and Crème Anglaise

Indulge in a delightful blend of Spanish flair and French elegance with Churros with Dark Chocolate Sauce and Crème Anglaise. Picture golden-brown churros, crispy on the outside and soft on the inside, served alongside a velvety dark chocolate sauce and a creamy crème anglaise. Each bite is a harmonious symphony of textures and flavors—a tribute to the vibrant streets of Spain and the chic cafes of France.

Ingredients

For the Churros

- 1 cup water
- 2 tablespoons sugar
- 1/2 teaspoon salt
- 2 tablespoons vegetable oil
- 1 cup all-purpose flour
- Vegetable oil, for frying

For the Dark Chocolate Sauce

- 1/2 cup dark chocolate chips
- 1/2 cup heavy cream
- 1 tablespoon unsalted butter

For the Crème Anglaise

- 1 cup whole milk
- 1/2 cup heavy cream
- 1/4 cup granulated sugar
- 4 large egg yolks
- 1 teaspoon vanilla extract

Instructions

For the Churros

1. In a saucepan, combine water, sugar, salt, and vegetable oil. Bring to a boil over medium heat.

2. Remove the saucepan from the heat and stir in the flour until the mixture forms a ball.

3. Heat vegetable oil in a deep skillet or pot to 375°F (190°C).

4. Transfer the churro dough to a pastry bag fitted with a large star tip.

5. Pipe 4-inch strips of dough into the hot oil, using scissors to cut them off. Fry until golden brown, about 2-3 minutes per side. Remove and drain on paper towels.

For the Dark Chocolate Sauce

1. In a small saucepan, heat the heavy cream until just simmering.

2. Remove from heat and pour over the dark chocolate chips in a heatproof bowl. Let it sit for a minute.

3. Add the butter to the chocolate mixture and stir until smooth and glossy.

For the Crème Anglaise

1. In a saucepan, heat the milk and cream over medium heat until just simmering.

2. In a separate bowl, whisk together the egg yolks and sugar until pale and thick.

3. Slowly pour the hot milk mixture into the egg yolk mixture, whisking constantly.

4. Return the mixture to the saucepan and cook over low heat, stirring constantly, until the custard thickens enough to coat the back of a spoon.

5. Remove from heat and stir in the vanilla extract. Strain the custard through a fine-mesh sieve.

Assembly

Serve the freshly fried churros with the warm dark chocolate sauce and the chilled crème anglaise for dipping.

Baba Ganoush Française

Baba Ganoush Française offers a delightful fusion of Middle Eastern tradition with French sophistication, epitomizing the culinary exchange that characterized Napoleon's era. This French-inspired rendition of the classic baba ganoush elevates the traditional eggplant dip with the nuanced flavors of Dijon mustard and extra virgin olive oil, resulting in a creamy and smoky spread that captivates the senses.

Ingredients

- 2 large eggplants
- 3 cloves garlic, minced
- 2 tablespoons extra virgin olive oil
- 2 tablespoons lemon juice
- 2 tablespoons Dijon mustard
- 2 tablespoons tahini
- Salt, to taste
- Black pepper, to taste
- Fresh parsley, chopped, for garnish
- French baguette or crackers, for serving

Instructions

1. Preheat the oven to 400°F (200°C).

2. Wash the eggplants and pat them dry. Prick the eggplants all over with a fork to prevent them from bursting while roasting.

3. Place the eggplants on a baking sheet lined with parchment paper. Roast in the preheated oven for about 45-50 minutes or until the eggplants are completely soft and collapsed.

4. Remove the eggplants from the oven and let them cool for a few minutes until they are cool enough to handle.

5. Once the eggplants are cool, slice them open lengthwise and scoop out the flesh into a bowl, leaving behind the skins. Discard the skins.

6. Using a fork or potato masher, mash the eggplant flesh until smooth and creamy.

7. Add minced garlic, extra virgin olive oil, lemon juice, Dijon mustard, and tahini to the mashed eggplant. Season with salt and black pepper to taste.

8. Mix all the ingredients until well combined. Adjust seasoning, if necessary, by adding more salt, pepper, or lemon juice to taste.

9. Transfer the Baba Ganoush Française to a serving dish and garnish with chopped fresh parsley.

10. Serve the Baba Ganoush Française with slices of French baguette or your favorite crackers.

Couscous Ratatouille

Couscous Ratatouille marries the comforting textures of North African couscous with the vibrant flavors of French ratatouille, resulting in a harmonious fusion that delights the palate and nourishes the soul. This recipe pays homage to the culinary traditions of both regions, where tender couscous grains embrace a medley of sautéed vegetables, aromatic herbs, and savory tomato-based sauce. A celebration of simplicity and abundance, Couscous Ratatouille invites you on a culinary journey that transcends borders, offering a taste of Mediterranean warmth and the timeless allure of French cuisine.

Ingredients

- 1 cup couscous
- 1 1/4 cups vegetable or chicken broth
- 2 tablespoons olive oil
- 1 onion, diced
- 2 cloves garlic, minced
- 1 eggplant, diced
- 1 zucchini, diced
- 1 yellow bell pepper, diced
- 1 red bell pepper, diced
- 2 tomatoes, diced
- 2 tablespoons tomato paste
- 1 teaspoon dried thyme
- 1 teaspoon dried oregano

- Salt and pepper, to taste
- Fresh parsley or basil, chopped, for garnish

Instructions

1. In a medium saucepan, bring the vegetable or chicken broth to a boil. Once boiling, remove from heat and stir in the couscous. Cover the saucepan and let it sit for about 5 minutes until the couscous absorbs the liquid. Fluff the couscous with a fork and set aside.

2. In a large skillet or sauté pan, heat the olive oil over medium heat. Add the diced onion and garlic, and cook until softened and fragrant, about 3-4 minutes.

3. Add the diced eggplant to the skillet and cook until it begins to soften, about 5 minutes.

4. Add the diced zucchini, yellow bell pepper, and red bell pepper to the skillet. Cook until the vegetables are tender but still slightly crisp, about 5-7 minutes.

5. Stir in the diced tomatoes, tomato paste, dried thyme, and dried oregano. Season with salt and pepper to taste. Cook for an additional 3-4 minutes, stirring occasionally, until the flavors meld together and the sauce thickens slightly.

6. To serve, fluff the couscous again with a fork and divide it among serving plates or bowls. Spoon the ratatouille mixture over the couscous.

7. Garnish the Couscous Ratatouille with freshly chopped parsley or basil. Serve hot.

Chicken Tagine with Preserved Lemon and Herbs

Chicken Tagine with Preserved Lemon and Herbs offers a tantalizing blend of Mediterranean flavors, merging the elegance of French cuisine with the aromatic richness of Egyptian culinary traditions. In this savory dish, tender chicken thighs are infused with fragrant herbs, warming spices, and the tangy brightness of preserved lemon, creating a symphony of flavors that dance on the palate. As the tagine simmers to perfection, it beckons you to savor the essence of two distinct culinary worlds converging in harmony.

Ingredients

- 4 chicken thighs, bone-in and skin-on
- 2 tablespoons olive oil
- 1 onion, finely chopped
- 3 cloves garlic, minced
- 1 teaspoon ground cumin
- 1 teaspoon ground coriander
- 1 teaspoon ground paprika
- 1/2 teaspoon ground cinnamon
- 1/4 teaspoon ground turmeric
- Salt and black pepper, to taste
- 1 preserved lemon, rinsed and thinly sliced
- 1 cup chicken broth
- 1 tablespoon honey
- Fresh parsley, chopped, for garnish
- Cooked couscous or rice, for serving

Instructions

1. In a large tagine or Dutch oven, heat the olive oil over medium heat. Add the chopped onion and minced garlic, and sauté until softened and fragrant, about 4-5 minutes.

2. Season the chicken thighs with ground cumin, ground coriander, ground paprika,

ground cinnamon, ground turmeric, salt, and black pepper.

3. Push the onion and garlic mixture to the side of the tagine and add the seasoned chicken thighs, skin-side down. Cook until golden brown, about 5-6 minutes.

4. Flip the chicken thighs over and add the sliced preserved lemon to the tagine, arranging them around the chicken.

5. Pour the chicken broth over the chicken thighs and preserved lemon slices. Drizzle the honey evenly over the chicken.

6. Cover the tagine and let it simmer over low heat for about 30-35 minutes, or until the chicken is cooked through and tender and the sauce has thickened slightly.

7. Once the chicken is cooked, remove the tagine from the heat. Sprinkle chopped fresh parsley over the chicken as a garnish.

8. Serve the Chicken Tagine with Preserved Lemon and Herbs hot, accompanied by cooked couscous or rice to soak up the flavorful sauce.

Lamb Kofta with Yogurt-Mint Sauce

Lamb Kofta with Yogurt-Mint Sauce combines the robust flavors of North African spices with the refreshing zest of Mediterranean herbs, resulting in a culinary fusion that captivates the senses. In this harmonious dish, succulent lamb is seasoned with aromatic spices, shaped into tender kofta, and grilled to perfection, evoking the warmth of Egyptian cuisine. Complemented by a creamy yogurt-mint sauce, each bite offers a tantalizing balance of savory and fresh notes, inviting you to savor the rich tapestry of flavors that bridge continents and cultures.

Ingredients

For the Lamb Kofta

- 1 lb ground lamb
- 1 small onion, grated
- 2 cloves garlic, minced
- 2 tablespoons fresh parsley, chopped
- 1 teaspoon ground cumin
- 1 teaspoon ground coriander
- 1/2 teaspoon ground cinnamon
- 1/4 teaspoon ground nutmeg
- 1/4 teaspoon cayenne pepper
- Salt and black pepper, to taste
- Olive oil, for grilling

For the Yogurt-Mint Sauce

- 1 cup Greek yogurt
- 2 tablespoons fresh mint leaves, chopped
- 1 tablespoon lemon juice

Instructions

1. In a large mixing bowl, combine the ground lamb, grated onion, minced garlic, chopped parsley, ground cumin, ground coriander, ground cinnamon, ground nutmeg, cayenne pepper, salt, and black pepper. Mix until well combined.

2. Divide the lamb mixture into equal portions and shape each portion into an oval-shaped kofta.

3. Preheat your grill or grill pan over medium-high heat. Brush the grates lightly with olive oil to prevent sticking.

4. Place the lamb kofta on the preheated grill and cook for about 4-5 minutes per side, or until they are cooked through and have nice grill marks.

5. While the lamb kofta are cooking, prepare the yogurt-mint sauce. In a small bowl, combine the Greek yogurt, chopped mint leaves, lemon juice, salt, and black pepper. Mix until well combined.

6. Once the lamb kofta are cooked, remove them from the grill and let them rest for a few minutes.

7. Serve the French-Egyptian Lamb Kofta hot, with the yogurt-mint sauce on the side for dipping.

8. Optionally, you can serve the lamb kofta with a side of couscous or rice pilaf and a fresh salad.

French Macarons with Pistachio and Rosewater

Egyptian-inspired French Macarons with Pistachio and Rosewater offer a captivating fusion of Middle Eastern allure and French sophistication. These delicate treats, inspired by the aromatic flavors of Egypt, combine the subtle nuttiness of pistachios with the floral essence of rosewater, encased in the airy perfection of French macaron shells. Each bite is a symphony of textures and tastes, inviting you to experience the harmonious blend of cultures and cuisines. With their vibrant hues and enchanting flavors, these macarons embody the timeless elegance of Egyptian cuisine and the refined artistry of French patisserie.

Ingredients

For the Macaron Shells

- 1 cup almond flour
- 1 3/4 cups confectioners' sugar
- 3 large egg whites, at room temperature
- 1/4 cup granulated sugar
- Green food coloring (optional)

For the Pistachio Rosewater Filling

- 1/2 cup unsalted butter, softened
- 1 1/2 cups confectioners' sugar
- 1/4 cup finely ground pistachios
- 1 teaspoon rosewater
- A few drops of green food coloring (optional)
- Crushed pistachios, for garnish

Instructions

For the Macaron Shells

1. Line baking sheets with parchment paper or silicone mats. Set aside.

2. In a food processor, pulse almond flour and confectioners' sugar until well combined and finely ground. Sift the mixture through a fine-mesh sieve into a large mixing bowl. Discard any large almond pieces.

3. In a separate mixing bowl, beat egg whites with an electric mixer until foamy. Gradually add granulated sugar, continuing to beat until stiff peaks form and the meringue is glossy. Optionally, add a few drops of green food coloring for a pistachio hue.

4. Gently fold the almond flour mixture into the meringue until just combined, being careful not to deflate the mixture. The batter should be smooth and flow like lava.

5. Transfer the macaron batter into a piping bag fitted with a round tip. Pipe small rounds (about 1-inch in diameter) onto the prepared baking sheets, leaving space between each macaron.

6. Let the piped macarons sit at room temperature for about 30 minutes to form a dry shell. Preheat the oven to 300°F (150°C) during this time.

7. Bake the macarons for 15-18 minutes, or until they have formed feet and the tops are set. Remove from the oven and let cool completely on the baking sheets before removing.

For the Pistachio Rosewater Filling

1. In a mixing bowl, beat softened butter until creamy and smooth.

2. Gradually add confectioners' sugar and beat until light and fluffy.

3. Stir in finely ground pistachios and rosewater until well combined. Add a few drops of green food coloring if desired.

4. Transfer the filling into a piping bag fitted with a round tip.

5. Pair up the cooled macaron shells based on size and shape.

6. Pipe a small amount of filling onto the flat side of one macaron shell, then sandwich with another shell.

7. Repeat with the remaining macaron shells and filling.

8. Optionally, roll the edges of the filled macarons in crushed pistachios for decoration.

9. Place the filled macarons in an airtight container and refrigerate for at least 24 hours to allow the flavors to meld.

10. Bring the macarons to room temperature before serving.

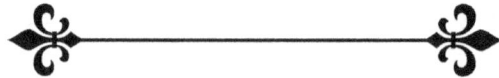

Schnitzel Cordon Bleu

Schnitzel Cordon Bleu embodies a harmonious fusion of flavors and techniques. It pays homage to the timeless appeal of German or Austrian schnitzel, a beloved classic characterized by its golden-brown crust and tender meat while embracing French Cordon Bleu's culinary finesse. Picture thinly pounded veal or pork cutlets enveloping a decadent filling of ham and Swiss cheese before being breaded and fried to crispy perfection. With each bite, the crisp exterior gives way to a symphony of textures and flavors, where the salty tang of ham harmonizes with the creamy richness of melted cheese.

Ingredients

- 4 boneless, skinless chicken breasts, pork loin slices or veal cutlets
- Salt and pepper, to taste
- 8 slices of ham (such as Black Forest ham or Virginia ham)
- 4 slices of Swiss cheese
- 1 cup all-purpose flour

- 2 large eggs, beaten
- 1 cup breadcrumbs
- Vegetable oil, for frying
- Toothpicks, for securing

Instructions

1. Prepare the Chicken/Pork: Place each chicken breast or pork loin slice between two sheets of plastic wrap. Use a meat mallet or rolling pin to pound the meat until it is about 1/4 inch thick. Season both sides of the meat with salt and pepper.

2. Assemble the Cordon Bleu: Lay 2 slices of ham and 1 slice of Swiss cheese on top of each pounded chicken breast or pork loin slice. Carefully roll up each piece, ensuring that the ham and cheese stay inside. Secure the rolls with toothpicks to prevent them from unraveling.

3. Coat the Schnitzels: Set up a breading station with three shallow bowls. Place the flour in one bowl, beaten eggs in another bowl, and breadcrumbs in the third bowl. Dredge each chicken or pork roll in the flour, shaking off any excess. Dip it into the beaten eggs, allowing any excess to drip off, then coat it evenly with breadcrumbs, pressing gently to adhere.

4. Fry the Schnitzels: In a large skillet, heat vegetable oil over medium-high heat until hot but not smoking. Carefully add the breaded chicken or pork rolls to the skillet, working in batches if necessary to avoid overcrowding. Cook until golden brown and crispy on all sides, about 3-4 minutes per side. Remove the Schnitzels from the skillet and place them on a paper towel-lined plate to drain excess oil.

5. Serve: Remove the toothpicks from the Schnitzels before serving. Serve hot with your favorite side dishes, such as mashed potatoes, salad, or steamed vegetables.

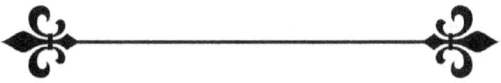

French Onion Soup with Pretzel Bread Croutons

In the realm of comforting soups that warm both body and soul, few dishes rival the timeless allure of French Onion Soup. Rooted in centuries of French culinary tradition, this soul-nourishing masterpiece marries the earthy sweetness of caramelized onions with the robust depth of savory broth, creating a symphony of flavors that captivates the palate. In this rendition, we elevate the classic by introducing a delightful twist—crispy pretzel bread croutons. Inspired by the German love affair with pretzels, these golden nuggets of toasted perfection add a crunchy dimension to the soup, offering a harmonious balance to its rich and hearty base. With each spoonful, the warmth of the broth mingles with the satisfying crunch of the croutons, inviting diners on a culinary journey that transcends borders and celebrates the timeless artistry of European cuisine.

Ingredients

- 4 large onions, thinly sliced
- 4 tablespoons unsalted butter
- 2 tablespoons olive oil
- 4 cups beef broth
- 2 cups chicken broth
- 1 cup dry white wine (optional)
- 2 cloves garlic, minced
- 1 teaspoon dried thyme
- Salt and black pepper, to taste
- 1 bay leaf
- 4 slices of pretzel bread, cubed
- 1 cup Gruyere cheese, shredded
- 1/4 cup Parmesan cheese, grated
- Fresh parsley, chopped (for garnish)

Instructions

1. Caramelize the Onions: In a large pot or Dutch oven, melt the butter and olive oil over medium heat. Add the thinly sliced onions and cook, stirring occasionally, until they are caramelized and golden brown, about 30-40 minutes.

2. Add Garlic and Thyme: Add the minced garlic and dried thyme to the caramelized onions. Cook for an additional 1-2 minutes until the garlic is fragrant.

3. Deglaze the Pot: If using, pour in the white wine to deglaze the pot, scraping up any browned bits from the bottom. Allow the wine to simmer for a few minutes until it reduces slightly.

4. Add Broth and Seasonings: Pour the beef broth and chicken broth into the pot with the caramelized onions. Add the bay leaf and season with salt and black pepper to taste. Bring the soup to a simmer and let it cook for another 20-30 minutes to allow the flavors to meld together.

5. Prepare the Pretzel Bread Croutons: Preheat the oven to 350°F (175°C). Spread the cubed pretzel bread on a baking sheet in a single layer. Toast the pretzel bread cubes in the oven for about 10-15 minutes until they are crispy and golden brown.

6. Assemble the Soup: Once the soup is ready, discard the bay leaf and ladle the hot soup into oven-safe bowls. Float a handful of toasted pretzel bread croutons on top of each bowl of soup.

7. Add Cheese and Broil: Sprinkle a generous amount of shredded Gruyere cheese over the pretzel bread croutons, followed by a sprinkle of grated Parmesan cheese.

8. Broil the Soup: Place the bowls of soup on a baking sheet and place them under the broiler for 2-3 minutes until the cheese is melted and bubbly and the edges are golden brown.

9. Garnish and Serve: Remove the soup from the broiler and garnish with freshly chopped parsley. Allow the soup to cool slightly before serving.

Croissant Strudel with Apple and Walnut Filling

Croissant Strudel with Apple and Walnut Filling marries French croissants' delicate flakiness with the Austrian strudel's rustic charm. This fusion of two beloved pastries captures the essence of European baking traditions, blending the buttery layers of croissants with the sweet and tangy allure of apple and walnut filling. Inspired by the picturesque orchards of Central Europe and the bustling patisseries of France, this indulgent treat embodies the harmonious union of flavors and textures. Each bite offers a symphony of sensations—a crisp exterior yielding layers of tender pastry enveloping a luscious medley of spiced apples and crunchy walnuts.

Ingredients

For the Filling

- 4 large apples (such as Granny Smith or Honeycrisp), peeled, cored, and thinly sliced
- 1/2 cup walnuts, chopped
- 1/4 cup brown sugar
- 1 teaspoon ground cinnamon
- 1/4 teaspoon ground nutmeg
- Zest of 1 lemon
- 2 tablespoons unsalted butter, melted
- 1 tablespoon all-purpose flour

For the Croissant Strudel

- 1 package of pre-made croissant dough (or homemade croissant dough)
- 2 tablespoons unsalted butter, melted
- Powdered sugar, for dusting (optional)
- Vanilla ice cream or whipped cream, for serving (optional)

Instructions

1. Preheat the Oven

- Preheat your oven to 375°F (190°C). Line a baking sheet with parchment paper or lightly grease it with butter.

2. Prepare the Filling

- In a large bowl, combine the sliced apples, chopped walnuts, brown sugar, ground cinnamon, ground nutmeg, lemon zest, melted butter, and all-purpose flour. Toss until the apples are evenly coated with the mixture.

3. Assemble the Croissant Strudel

- Unroll the pre-made croissant dough onto a lightly floured surface. If using homemade croissant dough, roll it out into a large rectangle.
- Arrange the apple and walnut filling evenly along the length of the dough, leaving about an inch of space along the edges.
- Gently roll up the dough, starting from the long edge, to enclose the filling. Seal the edges by pinching them together.
- Place the filled croissant strudel seam-side down on the prepared baking sheet.

4. Bake the Croissant Strudel

- Brush the top of the croissant strudel with the remaining melted butter.
- Bake in the preheated oven for 25-30 minutes, or until the croissant strudel is golden brown and the filling is bubbly.
- Remove from the oven and let it cool slightly before slicing.

5. Serve

- Dust the croissant strudel with powdered sugar, if desired.
- Slice the croissant strudel into pieces and serve warm.
- Optional: Serve with vanilla ice cream or whipped cream on the side for an extra indulgent treat.

Moules-Frites with Garlic Aioli

Moules-Frites with Garlic Aioli is a beloved dish revered for its simplicity and depth of flavor, epitomizing Belgian cuisine's coastal charm and culinary prowess. Delicately cooked in a fragrant broth infused with garlic, white wine, and fresh herbs, succulent mussels create a symphony of flavors that tantalize the taste buds and evoke memories of seaside dining. Paired with golden, crispy fries, a quintessential Belgian indulgence, the dish offers a delightful contrast in textures and a celebration of the country's rich culinary heritage. Elevating the experience is the creamy Garlic Aioli, a French-inspired condiment infused with the pungent aroma of garlic and the tangy richness of mayonnaise, adding depth and character to every dip.

Ingredients

For the Moules

- 2 kg (about 4.5 lbs) fresh mussels, cleaned and debearded
- 2 tablespoons unsalted butter
- 2 tablespoons olive oil
- 4 cloves garlic, minced
- 1 shallot, finely chopped
- 1 cup dry white wine
- 1/2 cup chicken or vegetable broth
- 1/4 cup chopped fresh parsley
- Salt and black pepper, to taste

For the Frites

- 4 large potatoes, peeled and cut into thick fries
- Vegetable oil, for frying
- Salt, to taste

For the Garlic Aioli

- 4 cloves garlic, minced
- 1/2 cup mayonnaise
1 tablespoon lemon juice
- Salt and black pepper, to taste

Instructions

1. Prepare the Moules (Mussels)

- In a large pot or Dutch oven, heat the butter and olive oil over medium heat. Add the minced garlic and shallot, and sauté until fragrant, about 1-2 minutes.
- Pour in the white wine and chicken or vegetable broth, and bring the mixture to a simmer.
- Add the cleaned mussels to the pot and cover with a lid. Cook for about 5-7 minutes, shaking the pot occasionally, until the mussels have opened.
- Discard any mussels that have not opened. Stir in the chopped parsley and season with salt and black pepper to taste.

2. Prepare the Frites

- Heat vegetable oil in a deep fryer or large pot to 350°F (175°C).
- Fry the potato fries in batches until they are golden brown and crispy, about 5-7 minutes per batch. Drain on paper towels and sprinkle with salt while still hot.

3. Prepare the Garlic Aioli

- In a small bowl, combine the minced garlic, mayonnaise, and lemon juice. Stir until well combined. Season with salt and black pepper to taste. Cover and refrigerate until ready to serve.

4. Serve

- Divide the Moules-Frites (mussels and fries) among serving bowls.
- Serve the Garlic Aioli on the side for dipping.
- Garnish the Moules-Frites with additional chopped parsley, if desired.
- Serve immediately, accompanied by crusty bread to soak up the delicious broth.

Belgian Waffles with Crème Fraîche and Berries

While Belgian waffles exude a rustic charm and undeniable allure, we infuse this classic treat with French finesse by adorning it with luxurious Crème Fraîche and a vibrant assortment of fresh berries. This fusion celebrates the harmonious marriage of two culinary worlds—the crispiness of Belgian waffles provides the perfect canvas for the creamy richness of Crème Fraîche, a staple in French cuisine. At the same time, the burst of flavor from ripe berries adds a delightful sweetness reminiscent of French patisseries.

Ingredients

- 2 cups all-purpose flour
- 2 tablespoons granulated sugar
- 1 tablespoon baking powder
- 1/2 teaspoon salt
- 2 large eggs, separated
- 1 3/4 cups milk
- 1/2 cup unsalted butter, melted
- 1 teaspoon vanilla extract
- Crème Fraîche, for serving
- Fresh berries (such as strawberries, blueberries, raspberries), for serving
- Maple syrup, for serving (optional)
- Powdered sugar, for dusting (optional)

Instructions

1. Preheat the Waffle Iron

- Preheat your waffle iron according to the manufacturer's instructions.

2. Prepare the Dry Ingredients

- In a large mixing bowl, whisk together the flour, sugar, baking powder, and salt until well combined.

3. Prepare the Wet Ingredients

- In a separate bowl, whisk together the egg yolks, milk, melted butter, and vanilla extract until smooth.

4. Combine Wet and Dry Ingredients

- Pour the wet ingredients into the bowl with the dry ingredients and stir until just combined. Do not overmix; some lumps are okay.

5. Whip the Egg Whites

- In another clean mixing bowl, beat the egg whites with a hand mixer or stand mixer until stiff peaks form.

6. Fold in the Egg Whites

- Gently fold the whipped egg whites into the waffle batter until just incorporated. Be careful not to deflate the egg whites too much.

7. Cook the Waffles

- Lightly grease the waffle iron with cooking spray or brush with melted butter.
- Pour enough batter onto the preheated waffle iron to cover the grids. Close the lid and cook according to the manufacturer's instructions until the waffles are golden brown and crisp.

8. Serve

- Once cooked, transfer the waffles to a serving plate and top each waffle with a dollop of Crème Fraîche and a generous serving of fresh berries.
- Drizzle with maple syrup, if desired, and dust with powdered sugar for an extra touch of sweetness.

Dutch-Style Croque Madame

Dutch-Style Croque Madame is a delightful fusion dish that offers a captivating blend of textures and tastes, where hearty slices of Gouda cheese and ham nestled between thick-cut white bread are elevated by the addition of Dutch-style mustard. What truly distinguishes this creation is the crowning glory of a perfectly cooked sunny-side-up egg, a nod to the beloved French Croque Madame.

Ingredients

- 8 slices of thick-cut white bread
- 8 slices of Gouda cheese
- 8 slices of ham
- 4 large eggs
- 4 tablespoons unsalted butter
- Dutch-style mustard, for serving
- Salt and pepper, to taste
- Chopped fresh parsley, for garnish (optional)

Instructions

1. Assemble the Sandwiches

- Lay out 4 slices of bread on a flat surface. Spread a thin layer of Dutch-style mustard on each slice.
- Place a slice of Gouda cheese on each slice of bread, followed by a slice of ham.
- Top each sandwich with another slice of bread to form 4 sandwiches in total.

2. Prepare the Croque Madame

- In a large skillet or griddle, melt 2 tablespoons of butter over medium heat. Once the butter is melted and the skillet is hot, carefully place the sandwiches in the skillet.
- Cook the sandwiches for about 2-3 minutes on each side, or until the bread is golden brown and the cheese is melted.
- Remove the sandwiches from the skillet and set them aside.

3. Cook the Eggs

- In the same skillet, melt the remaining 2 tablespoons of butter over medium heat.
- Crack the eggs into the skillet and season with salt and pepper.
- Cook the eggs sunny-side up until the whites are set but the yolks are still runny, about 3-4 minutes.

4. Assemble the Croque Madame

- Place a cooked egg on top of each sandwich.
- If desired, sprinkle chopped fresh parsley over the eggs for garnish.

5. Serve

- Serve the Dutch-Style Croque Madame immediately, while the eggs are still warm and the cheese is gooey.
- Optionally, serve with a side of Dutch-style mustard for dipping or spreading.

Pierogi with French Onion Sauce

Rooted in Eastern European tradition, pierogi encapsulate comfort and nostalgia, offering tender pockets of dough enveloping creamy mashed potatoes and savory cheese. Elevating this beloved dish to new heights is the addition of a luscious French Onion Sauce—a marriage of caramelized onions, velvety broth, and a hint of white wine, meticulously crafted to infuse each bite with layers of depth and complexity. This fusion of culinary worlds harmonizes the rustic simplicity of pierogi with the elegant allure of French gastronomy, inviting you on an adventure where tradition meets innovation, and every indulgent bite evokes the essence of cross-cultural culinary artistry.

Ingredients

For the Pierogi Dough

- 2 cups all-purpose flour, plus extra for dusting
- 1/2 teaspoon salt
- 1 large egg
- 1/2 cup sour cream
- 4 tablespoons unsalted butter, melted

For the Pierogi Filling

- 4 medium potatoes, peeled and diced
- 1 medium onion, finely chopped
- 1 cup grated cheddar cheese
- Salt and pepper, to taste

For the French Onion Sauce

- 4 large onions, thinly sliced
- 4 tablespoons unsalted butter
- 2 tablespoons all-purpose flour
- 2 cups beef or vegetable broth
- 1/2 cup dry white wine

Instructions

1. Prepare the Pierogi Dough

- In a large mixing bowl, combine the flour and salt. Make a well in the center and add the egg, sour cream, and melted butter.
- Gradually incorporate the wet ingredients into the flour until a dough forms.
- Turn the dough out onto a lightly floured surface and knead until smooth. Cover and let rest for 30 minutes.

2. Prepare the Pierogi Filling

- Boil the diced potatoes in salted water until tender. Drain and mash them in a large mixing bowl.
- In a skillet, sauté the chopped onion until caramelized. Add the caramelized onions to the mashed potatoes.
- Stir in the grated cheddar cheese and season with salt and pepper to taste. Set aside.

3. Form the Pierogi

- Roll out the dough on a floured surface to about 1/8-inch thickness. Use a round cookie cutter or drinking glass to cut out circles of dough.
- Place a spoonful of the potato filling in the center of each dough circle. Fold the dough over the filling and pinch the edges to seal, forming half-moon-shaped pierogi.

4. Cook the Pierogi

- Bring a large pot of salted water to a boil. Cook the pierogi in batches for about 3-4 minutes, or until they float to the surface. Remove with a slotted spoon and drain.

5. Prepare the French Onion Sauce

- In a large skillet, melt the butter over medium heat. Add the thinly sliced onions and cook until caramelized, about 20-25 minutes.
- Sprinkle the flour over the caramelized onions and cook for an additional 2 minutes, stirring constantly.
- Gradually pour in the beef or vegetable broth and white wine, stirring to combine. Simmer for 5-10 minutes, or until the sauce thickens. Season with salt and pepper to taste.

6. Serve

- Serve the cooked pierogi with the French onion sauce spooned over the top.
- Garnish with chopped parsley or chives, if desired.

Cabbage Rolls with French Tomato Sauce

Immerse yourself in a culinary experience where the humble charm of Eastern European cabbage rolls converges with the refined elegance of French gastronomy with this Cabbage Rolls with French Tomato Sauce recipe. Rooted in the heart of Eastern European kitchens, cabbage rolls offer a comforting embrace of tender cabbage leaves enveloping a savory filling of ground meat and rice. Elevating this beloved dish to new heights is the infusion of a French-inspired tomato sauce—a symphony of flavors crafted from ripe tomatoes, fragrant herbs, and aromatic spices.

Ingredients

For the Cabbage Rolls

- 1 large cabbage head
- 1 lb ground beef
- 1/2 lb ground pork
- 1 cup cooked rice
- 1 onion, finely chopped
- 2 cloves garlic, minced
- 1 egg, beaten
- 1 teaspoon paprika
- Salt and pepper, to taste

For the French Tomato Sauce

- 2 tablespoons olive oil
- 1 onion, finely chopped
- 2 cloves garlic, minced
- 1 can (28 oz) crushed tomatoes
- 1 tablespoon tomato paste
- 1 teaspoon dried thyme
- 1 teaspoon dried oregano

Instructions

1. Prepare the Cabbage Leaves

- Bring a large pot of salted water to a boil. Carefully remove the core from the cabbage head and place it in the boiling water.
- Cook for about 5-7 minutes, or until the outer leaves are tender and pliable. Remove the leaves and drain them on paper towels. Set aside.

2. Prepare the Filling

- In a large mixing bowl, combine the ground beef, ground pork, cooked rice, chopped onion, minced garlic, beaten egg, paprika, salt, and pepper. Mix until well combined.

3. Assemble the Cabbage Rolls

- Place a spoonful of the meat mixture onto the center of each cabbage leaf. Roll up the leaf, tucking in the sides, to form a cabbage roll. Repeat with the remaining filling and cabbage leaves.

4. Prepare the French Tomato Sauce

- In a large skillet, heat the olive oil over medium heat. Add the chopped onion and garlic, and sauté until softened and fragrant.
- Stir in the crushed tomatoes, tomato paste, dried thyme, dried oregano, salt, and pepper. Simmer the sauce for about 10-15 minutes, allowing the flavors to meld together.

5. Cook the Cabbage Rolls

- Preheat the oven to 350°F (175°C).
- Pour a thin layer of the tomato sauce into the bottom of a baking dish.
- Arrange the cabbage rolls in the dish, seam side down, in a single layer.
- Pour the remaining tomato sauce over the cabbage rolls, covering them completely.

6. Bake the Cabbage Rolls

- Cover the baking dish with aluminum foil and bake in the preheated oven for about 45-50 minutes, or until the cabbage rolls are cooked through and tender.

7. Serve

- Serve the cabbage rolls hot, spooning the French tomato sauce over the top.
- Garnish with fresh herbs, if desired.

Smørrebrød with French Cheese

Rooted in the heart of Scandinavian culinary heritage, Smørrebrød embodies simplicity and elegance, offering a canvas of dense rye bread adorned with an array of delectable toppings. In this delightful fusion, creamy French cheeses like Brie or Camembert take center stage, their velvety richness complementing the earthy texture of the rye bread. Layered with thinly sliced roast beef, smoked salmon, or pickled herring, these open-faced sandwiches offer a symphony of flavors and textures that tantalize the palate. Topped with crisp cucumber slices and radish rounds for a refreshing contrast, each bite promises a culinary adventure that transcends borders.

Ingredients

For the Smørrebrød

- Slices of dense rye bread or whole grain bread
- Butter or mayonnaise, for spreading
- Sliced French cheese (such as Brie or Camembert)
- Sliced roast beef, smoked salmon, or pickled herring
- Sliced cucumber
- Radish slices

- Fresh dill or parsley, for garnish
- Lemon wedges, for serving

Instructions

1. Prepare the Bread

- Toast the slices of rye bread until golden brown and crisp. Alternatively, you can use fresh slices of dense rye bread without toasting.

2. Spread the Base:

- Spread a thin layer of butter or mayonnaise on each slice of toasted bread.

3. Add the Toppings:

- Layer slices of French cheese (Brie or Camembert) on top of the buttered bread.
- Add slices of your preferred protein such as roast beef, smoked salmon, or pickled herring on top of the cheese.
- Arrange thinly sliced cucumber and radish slices over the protein.

4. Garnish and Serve

- Garnish the Smørrebrød with fresh dill or parsley leaves.
- Serve the open-faced sandwiches with lemon wedges on the side.

5. Variation

- For a vegetarian option, skip the meat and add sliced avocado, tomato, or boiled eggs as toppings.
- You can also experiment with different types of French cheeses such as goat cheese or blue cheese for unique flavor combinations.

6. Presentation

- Arrange the Smørrebrød on a serving platter or individual plates, and serve them as an elegant appetizer or light meal.

Scandinavian Seafood Bouillabaisse

Embark on a culinary odyssey where the elegance of French gastronomy meets the robust flavors of Scandinavian seafood in our enticing Scandinavian Seafood Bouillabaisse with a French Fusion Twist. Inspired by the legendary French bouillabaisse, this dish celebrates the marriage of French finesse with Nordic maritime heritage.

Ingredients

For the Bouillabaisse Base

- 2 tablespoons olive oil
- 1 onion, finely chopped
- 2 cloves garlic, minced
- 1 fennel bulb, thinly sliced
- 1 leek, sliced
- 2 carrots, peeled and diced
- 1 celery stalk, diced
- 1 can (14 oz) diced tomatoes
- 4 cups fish or seafood stock
- 1 cup dry white wine
- 2 bay leaves
- 1 teaspoon dried thyme
- Salt and pepper, to taste

For the Seafood

- 1 lb (450g) firm white fish fillets (such as cod or halibut), cut into chunks
- 1 lb (450g) mussels, cleaned and debearded
- 1 lb (450g) clams, cleaned
- 1/2 lb (225g) shrimp, peeled and deveined
- 1/2 lb (225g) scallops
- Fresh parsley, chopped, for garnish
- Crusty bread, for serving

Instructions

1. Prepare the Bouillabaisse Base

- Heat the olive oil in a large pot or Dutch oven over medium heat.
- Add the chopped onion and minced garlic. Sauté until softened and fragrant, about 3-4 minutes.
- Add the sliced fennel, leek, diced carrots, and celery. Cook, stirring occasionally, until the vegetables are tender, about 5-6 minutes.
- Pour in the diced tomatoes, fish or seafood stock, dry white wine, bay leaves, and dried thyme. Season with salt and pepper to taste.
- Bring the mixture to a boil, then reduce the heat to low. Simmer, uncovered, for about 20-25 minutes to allow the flavors to meld together.

2. Prepare the Seafood

- Once the bouillabaisse base is ready, add the chunks of white fish fillets to the pot. Cook for about 5 minutes, or until the fish is opaque and cooked through.
- Add the cleaned mussels and clams to the pot. Cover and cook for about 5-7 minutes, or until the shells have opened. Discard any mussels or clams that do not open.
- Stir in the peeled and deveined shrimp and scallops. Cook for an additional 2-3 minutes, or until the shrimp are pink and the scallops are opaque.
- Taste the bouillabaisse and adjust the seasoning with salt and pepper if needed.

3. Serve

- Ladle the Scandinavian Seafood Bouillabaisse into serving bowls.
- Garnish with freshly chopped parsley.
- Serve hot with crusty bread on the side for dipping and soaking up the delicious broth.

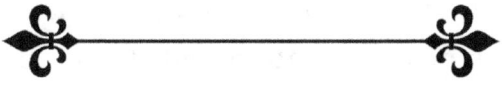

Epilogue

Napoleon Bonaparte, a name permanently carved into legend for his military prowess and visionary reforms, also wielded an unheralded culinary influence that transcended borders and was a testament to his global impact. Amidst the clash of armies and the redrawing of maps, the emperor's palate held a profound significance, weaving a tapestry of flavors that reached far beyond the battlefield. It was a conquest that went beyond sheer might and seeded a cultural exchange, a fusion of tastes, and a diplomatic language spoken at dinner tables rather than in negotiation chambers. Still, despite the indulgence and almost limitless options surrounding him, he held a soft spot for dishes that whispered of home and reminded him of his humble origins, connecting the emperor to the rustic flavors of his Corsican upbringing. Within this duality, the era blossomed into a delectable chapter of history.

As Napoleon's ambitions expanded beyond France's borders, so did the influence of French cuisine. Military campaigns reshaped maps and carried the essence of Gallic gastronomy to distant corners of the continent. As soldiers traversed the cobblestone streets of European cities and ventured into far-flung territories, they did not just carry weapons and banners; they bore the flavors and techniques of their native cuisine. These traditions found a new stage within the encampments' confines, where the armor clanking mingled with the enticing aromas. Here, army cooks wielded ladles and pans with as much finesse as soldiers wielding swords. In this tumultuous backdrop, the fusion of culinary cultures took shape—local ingredients intermingled with classic techniques, birthing a flavorful new landscape that transcended borders.

Moreover, the exchange of culinary practices was not a unilateral affair. Foreign influences found their way onto the French table, enriching chefs' repertoires and adding new dimensions to classic dishes. Fusing previously unknown ingredients, techniques, and culinary traditions sparked a revolution. It broadened the scope of French gastronomy—a departure from tradition that led to an era of creativity in the kitchen. Exotic spices, once rare and coveted, became part of the pantry, lending their aromas and flavors to traditional cuisine. The introduction of diverse vegetables, fruits, and herbs from conquered territories expanded the range of French chefs, allowing for a broader palette of flavors for exploration.

Amidst the intrigues of international relations and negotiating treaties, a subtler yet influential form of diplomacy quietly unfolded that transcended political boundaries. In Napoleon's era, the art of fine dining became a language spoken at dining tables, where the flavors of France served as ambassadors of goodwill. Banquet and state dinners became an arena for culinary diplomacy, where the artful presentations seduced foreign dignitaries and exquisite flavors crafted by French chefs were orchestrated to impress. Elaborate feasts, meticulously curated to showcase the finesse of French cooking, unfolded as strategic displays of cultural richness and sophistication. Napoleon, a master strategist on and off the battlefield, understood the persuasive power of gastronomic diplomacy. Each dish served became a nuanced statement—a subtle blend of flavors upon which bridges were built, alliances solidified, and cultural understanding fostered.

Restaurants around the globe pay homage to Napoleon's culinary legacy, offering menus that celebrate the elegance and sophistication of French gastronomy. From Michelin-starred establishments to cozy bistros, the principles of balance, precision, and attention to detail that defined the emperor's palate reverberate in exquisite dishes crafted by chefs today. Likewise, the fusion of flavors born from Napoleon's conquests lives on in the evolution of global cuisine. Dishes that embody the melding of French techniques with indigenous ingredients continue to captivate diners, offering a sensory journey through history and cultural exchange on a plate.

Napoleon's culinary legacy goes beyond the mere act of dining. It embodies the interconnectedness of cultures, the preservation of traditions, and the celebration of diversity. His influence on the gastronomic world stands as a testament to the enduring power of food to unite, inspire, and transcend time. This legacy continues to tantalize taste buds, spark innovation, and honor the artistry of a global culinary heritage.

"Everyone has loved me and hated me; everybody has taken me up, dropped me, and taken me up again.... Only this was not all at the same time but at intervals and at various periods. I was like the sun, which crossed the equator as it describes the ecliptics: as soon as I entered each man's clime, I kindled every hope, I was blessed, I was adored; but as soon as I left it, I no longer was understood and contrary sentiments replaced the old ones."[1]
~ Napoleon Bonaparte ~

Kitchen
CONVERSIONS

SPOONS & CUPS

tsp	tbsp	fl oz	cup	pint	quart	gallon
3	1	1/2	1/16	1/32	-	-
6	2	1	1/8	1/16	1/32	-
12	4	2	1/4	1/8	1/16	-
18	6	3	3/8	-	-	-
24	8	4	1/2	1/4	1/8	1/32
36	12	6	3/4		-	-
48	16	8	1	1/2	1/4	1/16
96	32	16	2	1	1/2	1/8
-	64	32	4	2	1	1/4
-	256	128	16	8	4	1

MILLILITERS
(ROUNDED TO THE CLOSEST EQUIVALENT)

tsp	ml
1/2	2.5
1	5

tbsp	ml
1	15

oz	ml
2	60
4	115
6	150
8	230
10	285
12	340

cup	ml
1/4	60
1/2	120
2/3	160
3/4	180
1	240

GRAMS
(ROUNDED TO THE CLOSEST EQUIVALENT)

oz	g	lb
2	56	-
4	114	-
6	170	-
8	226	1/2
12	340	-
16	454	1

• COOKING TEMPERATURES •

BEEF
RARE
120°-125°
MEDIUM RARE
130°-135°
MEDIUM
140°-145°
WELL
160°-165°

MEDIUM
140°-145°
MEDIUM WELL
150°-155°
WELL
160°-165°
PORK

FISH
145°

POULTRY
165°

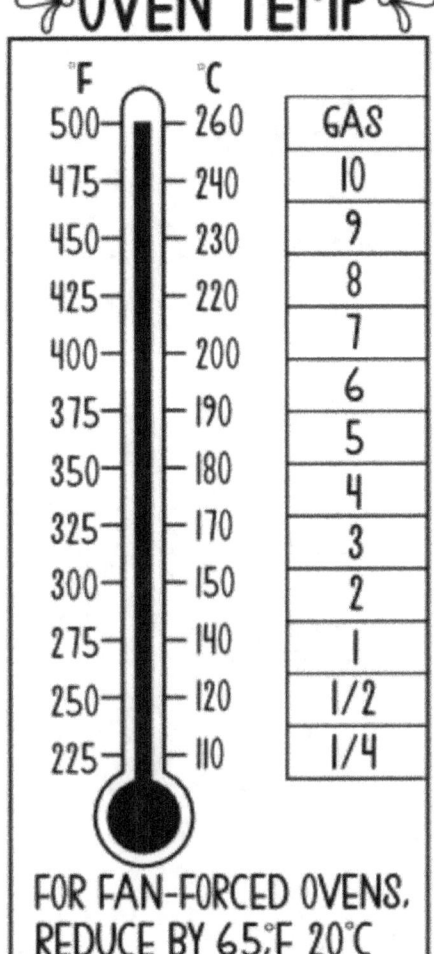

OVEN TEMP

°F	°C	GAS
500	260	10
475	240	9
450	230	8
425	220	7
400	200	6
375	190	5
350	180	4
325	170	3
300	150	2
275	140	1
250	120	1/2
225	110	1/4

FOR FAN-FORCED OVENS,
REDUCE BY 65°F 20°C

BUTTER
1 STICK
=1/2 CUP

HERBS
1 TBSP FRESH
= 1 TSP DRY

DASH = 1/16 TSP
PINCH= 1/8 TSP

Endnotes

Introduction

1. Napoleon Bonaparte, *The Mind of Napoleon: A Selection of His Written and Spoken Words,* Edited and translated by J. Christopher Herold (New York: Columbia University Press, 1961), 39.

Palate of Power

1. Andrew Uffindell, *Napoleon's Chicken Marengo: Creating the Myth of the Emperor's Favourite Dish* (Barnsley, England: Frontline Books, 2011), 74.

Rations and Resilience

1. Bonaparte, 219.

Epilogue

1. Bonaparte, 273.

Recipe Index

About the Author

Philine G. Lehmann is an educator turned author and entrepreneur. Armed with a BA in History and Political Science, a minor in Criminal Justice, an MA in History, and sixteen years of experience in the classroom, she is excited to bring her passion for the discipline to a larger audience through unique books and themed merchandise. She brings her depth of knowledge and outside-of-the-box thinking to each creative publication and product.

She lives in Westchester County, New York, with her husband, John, and her cat, Harley Quinn. In her free time, she enjoys ballroom dancing, visiting historical sites, collecting Baby Yoda/Grogu merch, cheering on her favorite teams, playing saxophone, and binge-watching classic movies and shows.

History Cafe Press is her lifelong dream, so follow along using the QR code below for updates on new book drops and swag releases.